VOLUME 2

GUIDE TO *Col* Wildflowers

D0373570

Mountains

Photography, watercolors
and text by G. K. Guennel

WESTCLIFFE PUBLISHERS

www.westcliffepublishers.com

*I respectfully dedicate this book to the memory
of my inspiring teachers at Butler University:
John E. Potzger and Ray C. Friesner.*

*"Oh my God! That's the
most beautiful thing
I've ever seen."*
— Hilde E. Guennel,
my loving and caring wife
of half a century, when
we found the exquisite
calypso orchid, the aptly
named Fairy Slipper.

International Standard Book Number: 1-56579-119-3

Library of Congress Catalog Number: 95-60672

Copyright:
G. K. Guennel, 1995. All Rights Reserved

Managing Editor:
Suzanne Venino, Westcliffe Publishers

Assistant Editors:
Dougald MacDonald
Sallie M. Greenwood

Design:
Rebecca Finkel, F + P Graphic Design

Published by:
Westcliffe Publishers, Inc.
P.O. Box 1261
Englewood, Colorado 80150
WWW.WESTCLIFFEPUBLISHERS.COM

Printed in Hong Kong by H & Y Printing Ltd.

For more information about other fine books and
calendars from Westcliffe Publishers, please contact
your local bookstore, call us at 1-800-523-3692,
write for our free color catalog, or visit us on the
Web at: **www.westcliffepublishers.com.**

Acknowledgments:
I owe special thanks to
Janet L. Wingate, Ph.D.,
and Loraine Yeatts of
the Kathryn Kalbach
Herbarium at the
Denver Botanic Gardens
who helped me with
identifications and,
hopefully, kept me
from making a fool
of myself. Any errors,
whatever their nature, are
mine and mine alone.

Introduction

During some thirty years of botanizing in Colorado, I used more than fifty books to identify plants. Apparently I was not alone. Friends and fellow hobbyists frequently expressed frustration in identifying plants, convincing me of the need for a comprehensive flower guide aimed at the layperson. The overwhelming need, expressed time and again, was for pictures, pictures, pictures.

The easiest way to identify an unknown plant is to compare it to a picture; the average person doesn't want or need botanical jargon. So when I started cataloging plants, I stressed color and pictures—painting watercolors and taking color photographs. The cliché "a picture is worth a thousand words" took on new meaning and real importance. It became a truism, and I became a true believer.

Although trained as a botanist, I consider my Colorado botanizing a hobby, for I earned my living dealing with fossil plants—primarily pollen and spores —not living ones. I relied heavily upon H. D. Harrington's *Manual of Plants of Colorado* (1964) and William A. Weber's two books, *Colorado Flora, Western Slope* (1987) and *Colorado Flora, Eastern Slope* (1990). Supplementing these "bibles" with many other sources, I was able to identify the plants I had collected and photographed over the years. The descriptive material that I extracted from these publications, I integrated with my own observations to compile the brief descriptions that accompany the watercolors and photographs.

Which species to include and how many was indeed a challenging question. Harrington lists 3,078 flowering plants and conifers, i.e., angiosperms and gymnosperms, respectively—far too many for a field guide with a description and two illustrations per species. I decided upon approximately 600 species that I consider to be fairly representative of what the average person might find.

The majority of plant species treated in these two volumes are wildflowers —flowering plants that grow in the wild. The term "wildflower" may be somewhat misleading, however, for this guide covers much more. While the average person may not recognize the reproductive structures of grasses and sedges as flowers, they are, nevertheless, flowers by definition, as are the reproductive organs of willow and cottonwood trees. I am, however, overstepping the boundaries of the term "flowers" when I include coniferous trees, such as pines and spruces. But if cottonwoods are covered here, why not blue spruces or bristlecone pines? They grow in the same places you find columbines and paintbrushes, and it would be hard not to notice them and be curious.

These two volumes are the culmination of some thirty years of study and research. With the pictures and text presented here, it is my hope that you will find enjoyment and satisfaction, as I have over the years, in discovering and identifying Colorado's wildflowers.

How to Use this Guide

An understanding of the overall organization of this guide will help you in identifying the flora of Colorado. First, it was necessary to divide the work into two volumes. Within each volume, I grouped plants by color, and then I split off trees/shrubs from herbs. Lastly, I listed the plants alphabetically by family, and within each family, alphabetically by common name. The explanations below elaborate more fully on this organization.

VOLUME 1 and VOLUME 2

Because of the sheer number and diversity of plants that grow in Colorado, this guide has been divided into two volumes. Volume 1 covers species you will most likely find in the plains and foothills—the life zones found between 3,500 and 8,000 feet in elevation. Volume 2 covers plants you will find in the mountains, above 8,000 feet, in the montane, subalpine, and alpine life zones. For more about Colorado's life zones, see pages 8–11.

COLOR

Within each volume, plants have been grouped by color for easy identification. A color bar on each page indicates whether you are in the green, white, yellow, red, blue, or purple section. Because color is the most obvious and striking characteristic of flowers, it makes sense to group them this way. There are, however, some drawbacks. What may appear red to me, may look orange to you. Or, a particular flower may be multi-colored, with white, purple, and red petals, and thus could be placed in three separate color sections. And what about species that produce individuals of different colors? Rosy paintbrush, for instance, can have pink, magenta, red, lavender, or purple bracts.

In order to keep these two books to a convenient size, it was necessary to select one color designation for each species. Keep in mind, however, that more than one color possibility may exist and that you may need to look for a given flower under more than one color. For example, if a flower is pink to lavender, look in this guide under red and purple.

The green section needs some explanation, since it is a catchall grouping for species that lack the more typical, showy colors associated with flowers. The flowering organs of grasses and sedges, as well as trees such as cottonwoods and willows, are basically green. Conifer trees—pines, spruces, firs, and junipers—have no flowers, yet their reproductive structures are primarily green or brown; these are included in the green section.

TREES/SHRUBS or HERBS

Most people can recognize a tree or a shrub by their large size and hard, woody stems and branches. Herbs, on the other hand, are neither woody nor large, but fleshy and generally small. I combined trees and shrubs into a single category (because they are relatively few in number) and arranged each color section so that the trees and shrubs appear first, followed by herbs. So if you were to come across a shrub with red flowers, you would turn to the red-tabbed pages and look at the beginning of that section under the TREES/SHRUBS heading. Conversely, if you came across a plant with red flowers that was obviously not a tree or a shrub, you would look in the red section under the HERBS heading.

Keep in mind, however, that there are trees and shrubs that are small in stature, such as the dwarfed willows and birches of the alpine zone. And there are herbs that reach ten feet in height. Nevertheless, I believe that creating one category for large, woody plants and another category for small, fleshy ones is a useful step in helping you locate a species in question.

PLANT FAMILIES

Species within the trees/shrubs heading are listed alphabetically by family, as are species under the herbs heading. A family represents a natural grouping of plants that are related through similar characteristics. Once you've chosen a color category and determined if an unknown flower is an herb, a tree, or a shrub, knowing the general family characteristics can prove helpful in deciding where to look in this guide.

If, for example, you can recognize a composite flower head, which is characteristic of the Aster family (a large family that includes daisies, sunflowers, goldenrods, and sages), you can limit your search to that family. Or, if you can identify a plant as a grass, or recognize the unique structure of a pea flower, then you can go directly to the alphabetical listings of those families. Thus the number of pages you need to flip through to compare an unknown flower to those in the book can be limited to one family at a time.

I believe I can guide you to a number of families simply by pointing out the more obvious characteristics of the larger families and the peculiarities of some of the others. Listed below are easily recognized families:

Aster family: composite flower heads *
Borage family: hairy appearance and tubular flowers
Cactus family: fleshy, leafless and spiny; with showy flowers
Celery family: flowers in umbels and compound, deeply dissected leaves
Evening Primrose family: long corolla tube, four petals, and eight stamens
Figwort family: two-sided flowers and opposite leaves
Grass family: green herbs with inconspicuous flowers and narrow leaves *

Knotweed family: hard, triangular fruit and knotlike nodes with papery sheaths
Mint family: square stems and aromatic, two-lipped flowers
Mustard family: four petals that form a cross
Pea family: beanlike seed pods; flowers with banner, keel, and two wings *
Rose family: five petals in radial symmetry and leaves in stipules
Sedge family: resembles grasses but have sharp, triangular stems
Willow family: all trees and shrubs, with catkins

See glossary for illustrations of these flower types.

SPECIES DESCRIPTIONS

Each page in this guide is devoted to a single plant species. The species
description consists of three components:

1. Common, Scientific, and Family Name
2. Plant Description
3. Habitat, Life Zones, and Flowering Time

Common, Scientific, and Family Name

Each wildflower in this guide is listed by its common name, which appears at the
top of the page in large, bold letters. It is in English and is the name often used
in the literature. It is not unusual for a flower to be known by more than one
common name. Alpine Fireweed, for instance, is also known as Low Fireweed,
Broadleaved Fireweed, Broadleaved Willowherb, Dwarf Fireweed, Red
Willowherb, and River Beauty. Alternate common names are listed in parentheses.

Below the common name is the plant's scientific name. Scientific names,
which are in Latin and are italicized, are based on an internationally accepted
system of nomenclature that identifies a plant species anywhere in the world.
While common names may be more descriptive, understandable, whimsical,
and pronounceable, they are not reliable; for the same common name may also
be applied to a number of different plants. I have followed William A. Weber's
nomenclature throughout this guide. After all, he is the guru of Colorado plant
taxonomy.

Most scientific names are binomials, that is, made up of two names. The
first name refers to the genus (capitalized) and the second refers to the species
(lowercased). For example, *Helianthus* (genus: sunflower) is combined with
pumilus (species: dwarf) to form the scientific name *Helianthus pumilus*. Some
scientific names are trinomials, should a species be split into subspecies.

Scientific names undergo changes from time to time. For example, a well-
established name may have to be abandoned if it is proven that the species in

question was described earlier under a different name, in which case, the older name has priority. Such name changes are governed by strict rules and documentation requirements. When a plant has had a history of previous scientific names, I have included them in parentheses below the currently accepted scientific name.

Following the common and scientific names is the name of the plant family, with its Latin equivalent in parentheses.

Plant Description

Next is an overall description of the plant, its general appearance, size, distinguishing characteristics, flowers, and leaves. This information has been extracted from the literature and was augmented by my own observations. I have tried to avoid botanical jargon and technical terminology wherever possible. When I could not avoid doing so, I have either explained the term within its context, included it in the glossary, or both.

Measurements are given in inches or feet, rather than in metric equivalents, because I believe the average person in the United States is not yet familiar with the metric system. Also, I have listed maximum dimensions—providing the upper limit of sizes instead of an average or an overall range.

Habitat, Life Zones, and Flowering Time

The last three items tell you where and when to look for the plant. Habitat is given first, listing the various environments in which the plant is found — whether it grows on rocky tundra slopes, for instance, or is more likely to be found along moist stream banks and lake shores. Again, I have added my own observations to information reported in the literature.

The range of life zones is listed next. Most wildflowers grow in more than one life zone. The common dandelion, for example, occurs in all five life zones: plains, foothills, montane, subalpine, and alpine.

Flowering time specifies the months when you will most likely find the flower in bloom. I have found the literature inadequate in citing such data, and in many instances I had to rely on my own observations. Keep in mind that flowering times are affected by elevation; plants growing at higher elevations will generally bloom later than the same species growing at lower elevations.

WATERCOLORS and PHOTOGRAPHS

Watercolors were drawn to scale but are printed in this book at approximately 75 to 80 percent of original size. Color photographs are not to scale; they show close-up details or the overall appearance of the plant.

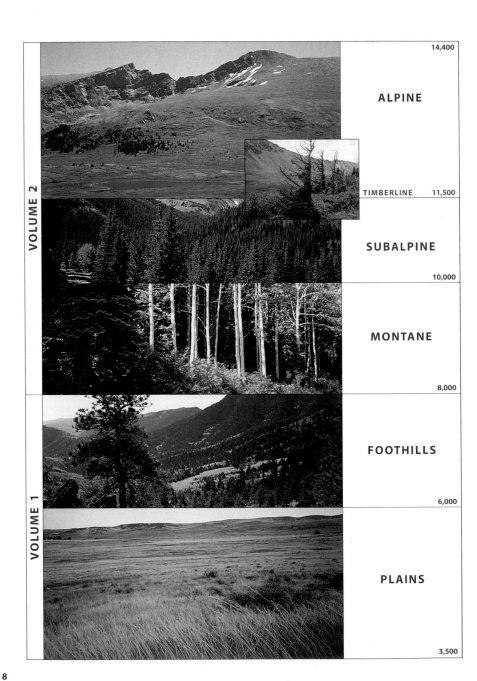

14,400

ALPINE

TIMBERLINE   11,500

SUBALPINE

10,000

MONTANE

8,000

FOOTHILLS

6,000

PLAINS

3,500

VOLUME 2

VOLUME 1

Colorado's Life Zones

Why a plant grows in a certain place is determined by many factors. Climate is the dominant influence; soil chemistry and biological factors are also important. In Colorado, topography and altitude are of particular significance, as there is an elevation of more than 11,000 vertical feet from the Great Plains to the summits of the Rocky Mountains.

Based on ecosystems and plant communities, and delineated by elevation, five distinct life zones have been defined in Colorado: the plains, foothills, montane, subalpine, and alpine zones. They correspond to the Sonoran, Transitional, Canadian, Hudsonian, and Arctic zones of the North American systems, which is based on latitude. In this comparison, where every 1,000 feet in elevation equals 600 miles in distance on the ground, driving from the town of Holly, Colorado, (elevation 3,386 feet) to the top of Mount Elbert (the state's highest peak at 14,433 feet) is the equivalent of traveling from Mexico to the Arctic Circle.

PLAINS ZONE — 3,500 to 6,000 Feet

Covering the eastern third of the state, the high plains of Colorado are primarily mixed-grass prairie, a grassland ecosystem. Where sandy hills or dunes interrupt the grassland, shrubs (sagebrush, rabbitbrush, snakeweed) take over, along with yucca and cacti. The trees of the plains (cottonwoods, willows, and boxelders) are restricted to streamsides and riverbanks. Although semi-arid, the plains are extremely rich in wildflowers. The Pawnee Buttes and Comanche Grasslands are especially noteworthy.

In the western part of the state, the equivalent of the plains life zone starts at about 4,500 feet on the Colorado Plateau. It is characterized by vast areas of sagebrush, shrubby desert plants, and sparse grasses. In spring and early summer, the slopes are aglow with bright wildflowers. Higher up pinyon-juniper association takes over.

FOOTHILLS ZONE — 6,000 to 8,000 Feet

In western Colorado, the pinyon-juniper association extends into the foothills. In eastern Colorado this zone is characterized by shrubs, dominated by scrub oak, mountain mahogany, three-leaf sumac, and common juniper. (The juniper of the western pinyon-juniper association is actually a cedar of the genus *Sabina*, not *Juniperus*.) Ponderosa pines, Douglas firs, blue spruces, and scattered aspens form open woodlands. Foothills flowers are abundant and diverse; too often transplanted by gardeners, they are literally being loved to death.

MONTANE ZONE — 8,000 to 10,000 Feet

The open woods of the foothills become a tighter, more cohesive forest in the montane. The addition of lodgepole and limber pines to the ponderosa pine-Douglas fir-blue spruce association, plus large aspen groves, give the montane zone a distinct look. The montane forest supports a rich understory of grasses and wildflowers. Shrubs grow in clearings and along the forests' edge. At the upper elevations of this zone, you find white fir (south of Colorado Springs) and bristlecone pine (south of Berthoud Pass).

The montane harbors large open areas known as mountain parks. North Park, Middle Park, South Park, and the San Luis Valley are vast meadows of grasses and sedges dotted with wildflowers. To see bistort, shooting star, little red elephant, or wild iris in such great profusion is a breathtaking experience.

SUBALPINE ZONE — 10,000 to 11,500 Feet

Dense forests of Engelmann spruce and subalpine fir dominate the subalpine zone. These tall, stately giants—they can reach 100 feet in height—form a distinctive dark green cape that drapes the shoulders of the mountain peaks. This is the zone of the hunters' "black timber," and the area carved up by ski slopes. Because showers are frequent and snow is sheltered by the dense growth of trees, water is abundant and forms pools, bogs, and swamps. Undergrowth, however, is sparse and limited to the forest edges and clearings. Along rivulets and in meadows, you find luxurious carpets of wildflowers. The dark, somber forest hides wood nymphs and Jacob's ladders, bog orchids and fairy slippers.

TIMBERLINE — About 11,500 Feet

Timberline—or treeline—is the boundary between the subalpine and alpine zones. Above this line the forests give way to tundra and trees no longer grow. Timberline is generally considered at 11,500 feet, although it is higher in the south (12,000 feet on Pikes Peak) and lower in the north (about 11,000 in Rocky Mountain National Park). It may zigzag up and down a few hundred feet in any given area, creeping upward on protected southern exposures and scooting down on cooler, north-facing slopes.

Harsh, drying winds and cold temperatures twist bristlecone pine and Engelmann spruce into stunted versions of those found at lower elevations. These misshapen trees, known as krummholz—German for "crooked wood"—are obvious indicators that you are at timberline.

ALPINE ZONE — 11,500 to 14,400 Feet

The treeless, windswept landscape of the alpine zone, the uppermost life zone, is commonly called tundra. Unlike the Siberian tundra, permanently frozen lowlands covered with mosses and lichens, the alpine tundra of Colorado is a high-altitude environment defined by sedges and grasses. Both environments are harsh and inhospitable.

The soils of the alpine zone are thin and porous, retaining little moisture. The sun's rays are strong, the winds fierce and relentless. Plants here have adapted to this severe environment. They grow low to the ground and protect themselves from heat, cold, and desiccating wind with cuticle and hair. By growing rapidly and producing seeds early, alpine plants not only manage to survive, but to thrive.

The sedges and grasses form a tight sod that anchors and holds the soil in place. Where the sedge/grass carpet is interrupted, dwarf shrubs move in and low herbs establish their own cushions and turf mats. Most alpine plants bloom in late June and early July, turning the alpine wasteland into a kaleidoscope of color.

Big Sagebrush
(Black Sage, Mountain Sagebrush, Wormwood, Mugwort)

Seriphidium tridentatum
(Artemisia tridentata)

Aster Family (Asteraceae)

Shrub, to 10' high, much-branched, with shredding bark.

Flower heads are many but small (about ¼" wide) and inconspicuous, silvery green.

Leaves are evergreen, strongly aromatic, to 1½" long, hairy beneath, with 3-toothed tips.

Grows in dry areas, such as hillsides, valley slopes, and deserts.

Life Zones: Plains to Subalpine

Flowering Time:
August and September

Hoary Sagebrush

(Hairy Sage)

Seriphidium canum
(Artemisia cana, A. viscidula)

Aster Family (Asteraceae)

Shrub, to 4' high, very aromatic, much-branched, with wiry, silvery twigs.

Flower heads are small (to ⅛"), green and brownish, and crowded into spikelike clusters that are up to 6" long.

Leaves are linear, to 2" long, silvery and hairy on both sides.

Grows in western Colorado, on sandy hillsides and in open woods, mountain parks, and meadows.

Life Zones: Foothills and Montane

Flowering Time: July to September

River Birch

(Rocky Mountain Birch,
Western Red Birch)

Betula fontinalis
(B. occidentalis)

Birch Family (Betulaceae)

Tree or shrub, to 25' tall, with
many stems and reddish brown
bark with lenticels.

Male catkins are cylindrical,
to 2½" long, and drooping;
the female catkins are oval,
less than 1" long.

Leaves are oval and toothed.

Grows in moist areas along
streams, ponds, and lakes,
and in canyons.

Life Zones: Foothills to Subalpine

Flowering Time: April to June

Rocky Mountain Alder

(Thinleaf Alder,
Mountain Alder)

Alnus incana tenuifolia

Birch Family (Betulaceae)

Tree or shrub, to 30' tall, branched at base, with scaly, gray to reddish bark.

Male and female flowers are on the same twig. The male catkins are drooping, to 3" long; female "cones" are less than ¾" long, woody, and persistent.

Leaves are oval, to 4" long, with prominent veins and toothed margins.

Prefers moist areas along streams, ponds, and lakes.

Life Zones: Foothills to Subalpine

Flowering Time: April and May

Common Juniper

(Ground Juniper, Mountain Juniper)

Juniperus communis alpina

Cypress Family (Cupressaceae)

Spreading shrub, to 3' high, in large patches, with scaly, light gray bark.

Cones are roundish, to ⅜" in diameter, and covered with blue bloom.

Needles are about ½" long, in whorls of 3, with sharp tips and white stripes on their upper surfaces.

Found on dry sites, such as hillsides, rocky slopes, forest clearings, and open woods.

Life Zones:
Foothills to Alpine

Pollination Time:
April to June

16

Red Cedar

(Western Red Cedar, Colorado Juniper, Rocky Mountain Juniper)

Sabina scopulorum
(Juniperus scopulorum)

Cypress Family (Cupressaceae)

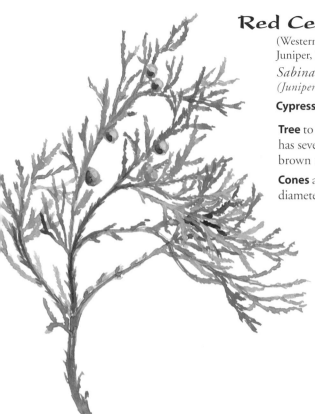

Tree to 50' tall or shrub that has several stems, with scaly, brown or gray bark.

Cones are berrylike, to ³⁄₁₆" in diameter, bluish, with 2 or 3 seeds.

Leaves are grayish green, to ³⁄₁₆" long, and scalelike (overlapping and hugging the twig).

Grows on hillsides, canyon walls, and cliffs in western Colorado and north of the Palmer Divide in eastern Colorado.

Life Zones:
Plains to Montane

Pollination Time:
April and May

Rocky Mountain Maple

(Mountain Maple, Dwarf Maple)

Acer glabrum trisectum

Maple Family (Aceraceae)

Small tree or shrub, to 20' tall, with smooth, gray stems and reddish brown twigs.

Flowers are tiny, greenish yellow, in clusters.

Leaves are opposite and palmately cut into sharply toothed lobes. The blades, to 3" wide, are borne by long, slender stalks and turn bright red in autumn.

Prefers moist places, such as stream banks, canyons, and north-facing slopes.

Life Zones:
Foothills and Montane

Flowering Time:
June and July

Douglas Fir
(Rocky Mountain Douglas Fir)

Pseudotsuga menziesii
(P. taxifolia, P. mucronata)

Pine Family (Pinaceae)

Stately tree, to 150' tall, with cylindrical crown, thick, furrowed, dark brown bark, and reddish brown branchlets.

Male cones are reddish; female cones are yellowish, to 4" long, with 3-pronged bracts protruding from the scales.

Needles are single, to 1¼" long, soft, flat, and blunt.

Grows in shady ravines and on rocky slopes where the soil is fairly deep.

Life Zones: Foothills to Subalpine

Pollination Time: April and May

Subalpine Fir

(Alpine Fir, Balsam Fir)

Abies lasiocarpa

Pine Family (Pinaceae)

Tall tree, to 100' high, with spire-like crown and light gray to grayish brown bark.

Male cones are cylindrical, to ¾" long, and dark blue; female cones are dark purple, to 4" long, with awl-tipped bracts.

Needles are flat, to 1½" long, with blunt, notched tips.

Prefers north-facing slopes and moist, cool sites along streams.

Life Zones: Montane and Subalpine

Pollination Time: May and June

White Fir

Abies concolor

Pine Family (Pinaceae)

Tall tree, to 100' high, with spirelike crown, straight trunk, and silvery bark.

Male cones to 1½" long, oblong, and reddish; female cones to 5" long, erect, cylindrical, and grayish green to purple.

Needles are single, broad, and flat, to 3" long, yellowish to silvery green.

Grows in moist canyons and on north-facing hillsides; limited to southern Colorado.

Life Zones: Foothills and Montane

Pollination Time: April to June

Bristlecone Pine

(Foxtail Pine)

Pinus aristata

Pine Family (Pinaceae)

Tree, to 45' tall, often twisted and stunted, with bushy crown, gray to brown bark, and bushy twigs.

Male cones are reddish, in clusters; female cones to 3½" long, reddish to dark purple, with sharp bristles on the scales.

Needles are in clusters of 5 (sometimes 3), less than 2" long, curved, sharp, dark green, with white resin spots.

Grows on rocky slopes and windy ridges. Some specimens have been dated at 2,000 years old.

Life Zones: Montane and Subalpine

Pollination Time: May and June

Limber Pine
Pinus flexilis
Pine Family (Pinaceae)

Tree, to 50' tall, with roundish crown, gnarled branches with upturned tips, and light gray to blackish brown bark.

Male cones are small and reddish; female cones are big (to 9" long), cylindrical, greenish brown, with thick, broad scales.

Needles are stout, in clusters of 5, to 3" long.

Commonly found on rocky or gravelly slopes, ridges, and peaks.

Life Zones: Foothills to Subalpine

Pollination Time: May and June

Lodgepole Pine

Pinus contorta latifolia

Pine Family (Pinaceae)

Slender tree, to 90' tall, in dense stands, with reddish to grayish bark.

Male cones are small and orange; female cones are reddish brown, lopsided, to 2" long.

Needles are stout, twisted, mostly in pairs, to 2½" long.

Grows on dry slopes and in burned areas.

Life Zones:
Foothills to Subalpine

Pollination Time:
May and June

Ponderosa Pine

(Western Yellow Pine, Rock Pine, Bull Pine)

Pinus ponderosa scopulorum

Pine Family (Pinaceae)

Sturdy tree, to 150' tall, with open crown and reddish bark.

Male cones are yellow, to 2" long; female cones are large (to 6" long), with woody scales that are prickle-tipped.

Needles are in pairs or threes, to 6" long, yellowish green, stiff, and sharply pointed.

Grows on exposed hillsides, mesas, and south-facing slopes.

Life Zones: Foothills and Montane

Pollination Time: April and May

Colorado Blue Spruce

Picea pungens

Pine Family (Pinaceae)

Stately tree, to 100' tall, with conical crown, gray bark, and bluish needles; the young branches are reddish.

Male cones are small, to ½" long, and orange; female cones are light brown, to 5" long, and pendant.

Needles are stiff, very sharp, to 1¼" long, and bluish green.

Grows in moist valleys, canyons, and on stream banks. This majestic giant is Colorado's state tree.

Life Zones: Foothills and Montane

Pollination Time: April and May

Englemann Spruce
Picea engelmannii

Pine Family (Pinaceae)

Tall tree, to 100' high, narrow, steeple-shaped, with straight trunk and scaly, reddish brown bark.

Male cones are cylindrical, about ½" long; female cones are 2½" long, pendant, with tooth-tipped scales.

Needles are short, about ¾" long, angular, curved, and thick, with sharp tips.

Found as tall, straight, narrow beauties on north slopes and in sheltered canyons, and as krummholz at timberline.

Life Zones: Montane and Subalpine

Pollination Time: May and June

Aspen

(Quaking Aspen)

Populus tremuloides

Willow Family (Salicaceae)

Tree, to 60' tall, with smooth, whitish bark. Forms groves via suckers.

Male and female catkins are on separate trees; both are pendant.

Leaves are small (to 3" long), roundish, on long, flattened stalks.

Prefers moist slopes and stream banks, but also invades avalanche gullies and burned areas.

Life Zones: Foothills to Subalpine

Flowering Time: April to June

28

Narrowleaf Cottonwood

Populus angustifolia

Willow Family (Salicaceae)

Medium tree, to 60' tall, with pyramid-shaped crown, dark gray, fissured trunk, and whitish, smooth bark.

Male and female catkins are on separate trees; both are about 2" long.

Leaves are lance-shaped, to 4" long, shiny green above, and pale below, with pointed tips and toothed margins.

Prefers moist sites, such as floodplains, and river and stream banks.

Life Zones:
Foothills and Montane

Flowering Time:
April to June

Arctic Willow

(Rock Willow)

Salix arctica
(S. anglorum)

Willow Family (Salicaceae)

Dwarf shrub, to 8" high, with creeping stems and branches.

Female catkins are large, to 1½" long; male catkins are small (less than ½" long).

Leaves are small (less than 1½" long), dark green above, and pale beneath.

Grows in wet places, such as lake shores, stream banks, and meadows, but also on rocky slopes.

Life Zones: Subalpine and Alpine

Flowering Time: July and August

Blue Willow

Salix drummondiana
(S. subcoerulea)

Willow Family (Salicaceae)

Tall shrub, to 10' high; the twigs are covered with whitish to bluish bloom.

Male and female catkins are both about 1¼" long, tinged red.

Leaves are about 1½" long, tapering in both directions, hairy beneath.

Grows in wet areas, such as pond and lake shores, stream banks, and meadows.

Life Zones:
Foothills to Subalpine

Flowering Time:
April to June

Planeleaf Willow

(Plainleaf Willow, Winter Candle)

Salix planifolia
(S. chlorophylla, S. phylicifolia)

Willow Family (Salicaceae)

Shrub, to 9' tall (less than 3' tall above timberline), in thickets, with shiny, maroon twigs.

Female catkins are dense, to 2" long; male catkins are less than 1" long and have reddish to purplish anthers.

Leaves to 2¾" long, elliptical or oval, dull green above, and whitish beneath.

Grows in moist areas, such as bogs, swamps, lake shores, meadows, and stream banks.

Life Zones: Foothills to Alpine

Flowering Time: June to August

Scouler Willow

Salix scouleriana
(S. flavescens, S. nuttallii)

Willow Family (Salicaceae)

Tree or shrub, to 25' high, with drooping branches and reddish to purplish twigs.

The male catkins are about 1" long; female catkins are 2" or more long. Fruit is blackish, hairy, and beaked.

Leaves are narrowly oval, to 5" long and 1½" wide, dark green and shiny above, pale beneath, with reddish hairs, yellow veins, and round-toothed margins.

Grows along forest borders and in clearings, but mostly on stream banks and lake shores.

Life Zones: Foothills to Subalpine

Flowering Time: May and June

Short-Fruited Willow

(Barrenground Willow, Grayleaf Willow)

Salix brachycarpa
(S. glauca)

Willow Family (Salicaceae)

Erect or creeping shrub,
to 6' high, thicket-forming,
with short, stout branches.

Female catkins are less than
¾" long and roundish; male
catkins are short (less than
½" long), with yellow to
reddish anthers.

Leaves are pale bluish green
on top, whitish and woolly
beneath, to 1½" long.

Grows in wet meadows and
along streams and ponds.

Life Zones: Foothills to Alpine

Flowering Time: June to August

Snow Willow

(Rocky Mountain Snow Willow)

Salix reticulata nivalis
(S. nivalis)

Willow Family (Salicaceae)

Dwarf shrub, to 6" high, with thick, blackish brown stems and branches.

Female catkins are small, to ½" long; male catkins are lesss than ¼" long, with dark red anthers.

Leaves are small (to 1" long), smooth, dark green above, and grayish below, with prominent veins in a netlike pattern.

Grows in meadows and on talus, rocky ledges, and tundra slopes.

Life Zones: Subalpine and Alpine

Flowering Time: July and August

Alpine Mountain Sage

(Patterson's Sagewort, Alpine Sage)

Artemisia pattersonii

Aster Family (Asteraceae)

Perennial, to 8" tall, with erect, unbranched, woolly stems; several stems grow from one rootstock.

Flower heads are small (to ⅜" across), as many as 4 per stem, with hairy tufts and brown-rimmed bracts.

Leaves are grayish, densely hairy, and pinnately divided into narrow lobes; basal leaves are stalked, to 2" long.

Grows on grassy slopes and rocky tundra, and among boulders.

Life Zone: Alpine

Flowering Time: July and August

Arctic Sage
(Mountain Sagewort, Norway Sagewort, Boreal Mountain Sage)

Artemisia arctica saxicola
(A. norvegica)

Aster Family (Asteraceae)

Perennial, to 12" high, in clumps, with downy, reddish stems.

Flower heads are in a leafy raceme, with short stalks; bracts are green and white, with brown, papery margins.

Leaves are divided 3 times, into narrow, pointed lobes that are grayish, silky, and fleshy.

Common on rocky slopes, boulder fields, and grassy tundra.

Life Zone: Alpine

Flowering Time: July and August

Boreal Sage

(Boreal Sagewort, Field Sage)

Oligosporus groenlandicus
(Artemisia borealis, A. campestris)

Aster Family (Asteraceae)

Perennial, to 20" high, in clumps, with deep taproot and reddish, stout, smooth stems.

Flower heads are in a spikelike, leafy raceme, with no ray flowers; disk flowers are brownish red, and bracts are green and purplish.

Leaves are mostly basal and divided into narrow, pointed lobes; leaves have long stalks.

Grows in sandy or gravelly disturbed areas, such as trailsides, tundra slopes, and hillsides.

Life Zones: Subalpine and Alpine

Flowering Time: July and August

Bracken Fern

(Bracken, Brake, Pasture Brake, Hog Brake)

Pteridium aquilinum lanuginosum

Bracken Family (Hypolepidaceae)

Perennial, to 5' high, with deep rootstocks; forms large colonies.

Spore cases are hidden by the rolled-up margins of the leaflets.

Leaves (fronds) are divided 3 times; the ultimate segments are about ½" long, leathery, dark green on top, and cobwebby beneath.

Commonly found in open woods, aspen groves, clearings, and burns.

Life Zones: Foothills and Montane

Sporing Times: July and August

Alpine Timothy

Phleum commutatum
(P. alpinum)

Grass Family (Poaceae)

Perennial, to 2' tall, tightly tufted, with smooth, wiry, erect stem, from creeping base.

Flowers are in form of a spikelike panicle that is plump, dense, purplish, to 2" long, with ³⁄₁₆" long spikelets. Glumes are awned, with green keels and hyaline margins.

Leaves to 4" long, ¼" wide, with inflated sheaths.

Common in wet areas, such as bogs, meadows, stream banks, and forest borders.

Life Zones: Subalpine and Alpine

Flowering Time: July and August

Foxtail Barley

(Ticklegrass, Squirreltail, Wild Barley)

Critesion jubatum
(Hordeum jubatum)

Grass Family (Poaceae)

Tufted perennial, to 30" tall, erect or leaning.

Flowers are in purplish brown spikelets, with 3" awns; spikes are bunched into one-sided, nodding, 4" long clusters.

Leaves are flat, rough, hairy beneath, to 6" long.

Abundant in waste places, open ground, ditches, meadows, and prairies.

Life Zones: Plains to Montane

Flowering Time: June to August

Perennial Brome

(Smooth Brome)

Bromopsis inermis pumpelliana

Grass Family (Poaceae)

Perennial, to 4' tall, with creeping rootstock and ascending branches in bundles.

Flowers are in spikelets, to 1⅜" long, and purplish green; spikelets form long (to 8"), narrow panicle.

Leaves are hairy, to 12" long, ⁵⁄₁₆" wide.

Grows in fields and ditches, and along roadsides and the edges of woods; Eurasian import.

Life Zones: Plains to Subalpine

Flowering Time: June to August

Spike Trisetum

Trisetum spicatum
(T. majus, T. subspicatum)

Grass Family (Poaceae)

Flowers are in form of a spikelike panicle, to 6" long, dense, shaggy, purplish to yellow, with protruding awns that are ³⁄₁₆" long, twisted, and spreading. Spikelets are 2-flowered, with 2 glumes and 2 awned lemmas.

Leaves to 6" long, ³⁄₁₆" wide, flat or inrolled.

Abundant on gravelly slopes and ridges, and in meadows and forest clearings.

Life Zones: Montane to Alpine

Flowering Time: June to August

Timber Oatgrass

Danthonia intermedia

Grass Family (Poaceae)

Perennial, to 10" high, densely tufted, with bright green, stout stem.

Flowers are in a narrow panicle, to 1½" long, with up to 8 spikelets on ascending stalks. Flower has long, papery, green and purplish glumes and lemmas with flat, ⅜" long awns.

Leaves to 6" long, ³⁄₁₆" wide, with flat or inrolled margins.

Grows in meadows and forest openings, near bogs, and on talus slopes.

Life Zones: Montane to Alpine

Flowering Time: July to September

Common Horsetail

(Field Horsetail)

Equisetum arvense

Horsetail Family (Equisetaceae)

Perennial, with rootstock.

Fertile stems are slender, to 2' high, with 1½" cones at the tips. Sterile stems are taller, to 32", 4-angled, and branched at 1" intervals.

Brushy branches serve as leaves.

Grows in wet locations, such as ditches, stream banks, meadows, and flood plains, but also along roads and railroad tracks.

Life Zones: Plains to Subalpine

Sporing Time: April to June

Smooth Scouring Rush

Hippochaete laevigata
(Equisetum laevigatum)

Horsetail Family
(Equisetaceae)

Perennial, with rootstock.

The sterile stems are erect, curved, much-branched, to 4' long; the fertile stems are erect, to 30" high, with ⅝" cones at the tips.

Stringlike branches serve as leaves.

Grows in moist environments, such as ditches, stream banks, and pond shores.

Life Zones: Plains to Subalpine

Sporing Time: April to June

Willow Dock

Rumex triangulivalvis
(R. mexicanus, R. salicifolius)

Knotweed Family (Polygonaceae)

Perennial, with taproot and erect stem to 30" high, branched near top.

Flowers are small, greenish or brownish, arranged in cylindrical clusters.

Leaves are narrow, to 6" long, with wavy margins.

Common in meadows, along streams and roads, and in open woods.

Life Zones: Foothills to Subalpine

Flowering Time: June to August

Green Bog Orchid

(New Mexico Bog Orchid, Purple Bog Orchid)

Limnorchis saccata
(L. neomexicana, L. purpurescens,
L. stricta, Habenaria saccata)

Orchid Family (Orchidaceae)

Perennial, to 2' tall, with tuberous root and erect, stout, unbranched stem.

Flowers are in dense spikes to 5" long, with 3 green sepals (the upper one a spurred hood) and 3 whitish, greenish, brownish, and purplish petals. The middle petal (the lip) exceeds the sac-like spur.

Leaves are parallel-veined, to 6" long, fleshy, with pointed, tapering tips.

Grows in wet, shady places, such as bogs, swamps, meadows, and forests.

Life Zones: Montane and Subalpine

Flowering Time: July to September

Northern Green Orchid

(Green Orchid, Green Rein Orchid,
 Leafy Green Orchid)

Limnorchis hyperborea
(L. viridiflora, Habenaria hyperborea,
 Planthera hyperborea)

Orchid Family (Orchidaceae)

Perennial, to 2' tall, with tuberous roots
and stout stem.

Flowers are in tight spikes, to 5" long.
The 3 sepals are petal-like, and one forms
a hood; the 3 petals are greenish, whitish,
or even reddish, and one is spurred.

Leaves to 6" long and parallel-veined;
leaves hug the stem.

Found in wet, shady places, such as bogs,
swamps, ditches, stream banks, and forests.

Life Zones: Montane and Subalpine

Flowering Time: June to August

Chestnut Rush

Juncus castaneus

Rush Family (Juncaceae)

Perennial, to 18" high, in bunches, with erect, stiff, round, smooth, and dark green stems; propagates via underground stems.

Flowers are in 3 clusters, each about ⅜" long, and dark brown.

Leaves are basal, erect, and channeled.

Found in wet meadows and bogs, and along streams and lakes.

Life Zones: Subalpine and Alpine

Flowering Time: July and August

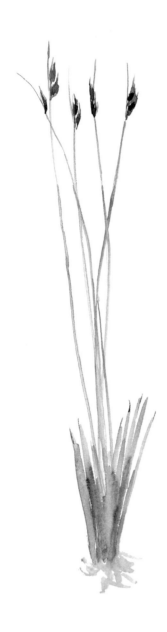

Drummond's Rush

Juncus drummondii
(J. subtriflorus)

Rush Family (Juncaceae)

Perennial, in tufts, with leafless stems, to 10" high, that are smooth, round, deep green, and have a pointed tip that is taller than the flowers.

Flowers (2 or 3) are brownish, with whitish sepals and shiny, brown fruits.

Leaves are few, basal, as long as the stems.

Common along streams and lakes, and in wet depressions and tundra.

Life Zones: Subalpine and Alpine

Flowering Time: July and August

Rocky Mountain Rush

Juncus saximontanus
(J. parous, J. brunnescens)

Rush Family (Juncaceae)

Perennial, to 18" tall, in tufts, with creeping rootstock and erect or leaning stems.

Flowers are small (³⁄₁₆" long), in a few dense clusters at the top of the stem. Flowers have 3 broad, tan sepals and 3 narrow, pointed, dark brown petals.

Leaves are sword-shaped, to ⅛" wide, and flattened; the sheaths are translucent.

Grows in wet places, such as swamps, bogs, and lake shores.

Life Zones: Plains to Subalpine

Flowering Time: July and August

Spiked Woodrush

Luzula spicata
(Juncoides spicatum)

Rush Family (Juncaceae)

Perennial, to 16" tall, forming tough tussocks, with erect, hollow stems.

Flowers form a compact, brown, roundish, spikelike cluster that is up to 1" long and subtended by a fierce, sharply spiked bract.

Leaves are flat, to ³⁄₁₆" wide, basal.

Grows on slopes and grassy tundra.

Life Zone: Subalpine and Alpine

Flowering Time: July and August

Kobresia

Kobresia myosuroides
(K. bellardi, Elyna bellardi)

Sedge Family (Cyperaceae)

Perennial, to 16" tall, with slender, triangular stems, in dense tufts that form hummocks.

Flowers are differentiated by sex and paired in a spikelet; several spikelets form a slender terminal spike, to 1" long.

Leaves are threadlike, with brown sheaths; leaves turn orange in autumn.

Grows in moist places on peaty tundra and along pond shores, as well as on wind-swept peaks and ridges. Kobresia is considered to be the climax vegetation of mature tundra.

Life Zone: Alpine

Flowering Time: July to September

Black Sedge

Carex ebenea
(C. haydeniana ebenea)

Sedge Family (Cyperaceae)

Perennial, to 20" tall, in tufts, with erect, triangular stems extending above the leaves.

Flowers are in ½" long spikes (female flowers on top) forming a dense terminal cluster. Flowers have black scales.

Leaves (to 5 per stem) are basal, ⅛" wide, firm, and flat.

Common along roads and in clearings and meadows.

Life Zones: Montane to Alpine

Flowering Time: July to September

Narrow-Leaved Sedge

Carex stenophylla eleocharis
(C. eleocharis)

Sedge Family (Cyperaceae)

Perennial, to 8" tall, in tufts, with slender, creeping rootstock and smooth, erect stems.

Flowers are in spikes (to 7), in tight, ⅝" long head, with male spikes at top and female spikes below, and brown and white scales.

Leaves are narrow, erect or arching, with stiff sheaths. Each stem has 4 leaves.

Common in open areas, on grassy slopes and dry prairies, and along roads.

Life Zones: Plains to Subalpine

Flowering Time: June to August

Narrow-Winged Sedge

Carex microptera

Sedge Family (Cyperaceae)

Perennial, to 40" tall, in tight tufts, with erect, triangular stems.

Flowers are in ¾" spikes that form a dense terminal cluster with a female spike at the top. Flowers have oval, dull brown scales and awned bracts with narrow margins.

Leaves (5 per stem) are flat, firm, to ³⁄₁₆" wide.

Common in open areas on slopes and stream banks, and in woods and meadows.

Life Zones: Foothills and Montane

Flowering Time: July and August

New Sedge

Carex nova
(C. nova erxlebenii, C. melanocephala,
* C. violacea)*

Sedge Family (Cyperaceae)

Tufted, to 2' tall, with creeping root-stock and erect, stiff stems that exceed the leaves and have reddish bases.

Flowers form spikes (as many as 4) in a tight cluster, to ¾" long, that is sub-tended by a long bract. The scales are reddish black, with translucent margins.

Leaves (to 15) are basal, firm, erect, to ³⁄₁₆" wide. Old, brown leaves are conspicuous.

Common in moist areas in meadows, near springs, and along streams.

Life Zones: Montane to Alpine

Flowering Time: July to September

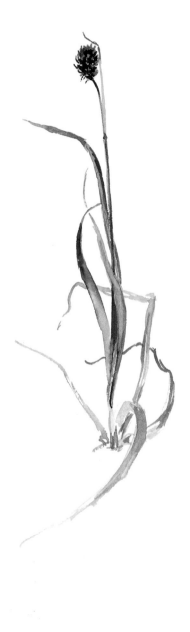

Rock Sedge
(Curly Sedge)

Carex rupestris drummondiana
(C. drummondiana)

Sedge Family (Cyperaceae)

Perennial, to 6" tall, with stout, erect stems in loose tufts and with conspicuous old leaves.

Flowers are arranged in a single, 1" long, terminal spike, with male flowers making up the upper ⅔. Scales are brownish to purplish, with translucent margins.

Leaves (about 12 per plant) are basal, ⅛" wide, with withering, curled tips.

Common in exposed sites, such as summits, rocky ridges, gravelly slopes, and tundra.

Life Zones: Subalpine and Alpine

Flowering Time: July to September

Rocky Mountain Sedge
Carex scopulorum

Sedge Family (Cyperaceae)

Perennial, to 16" tall, tussock-forming, with purplish, stout, creeping rootstock and stiff, erect stalks.

Male flower spike is terminal, slender, to 1" long; the female spikes (as many as 6) also are 1" long but oval. Bracts are scalelike and black-eared; scales are oval, purplish black.

Leaves (to 15) are basal, about ¼" wide, bright green, thick, and flat. Old leaves are conspicuous, truncated.

Very common in wet areas, such as pond and stream banks, meadows, seeps, and tundra depressions.

Life Zones: Subalpine and Alpine

Flowering Time: July to September

Mountain Balm

(Sticky Laurel, Snowbrush,
 Deerbrush, Mountain Laurel,
 Tobaccobrush, Soapbloom)

Ceanothus velutinus velutinus

Buckthorn Family
(Rhamnaceae)

Shrub, to 5' high but often prostrate, in dense patches, with grayish green bark.

Flowers are tiny, white, in large, dense clusters.

Leaves are alternate, evergreen, to 3¼" long, thick, leathery, and finely toothed.

Common on hillsides, in draws and burned areas, and along roadsides.

Life Zones:
Foothills and Montane

Flowering Time:
June to August

Red Prickly Currant

(Prickly Currant, Alpine Prickly Currant,
Subalpine Prickly Currant, Red Prickly
Gooseberry, Red-Fruited Gooseberry)

Ribes montigenum
(R. lentum, Limnobotrya montigena)

Gooseberry Family (Grossulariaceae)

Shrub, to 2' high, with spreading,
spiny, sticky branches. Spines, at leaf
bases, are numerous, slender, and sharp.

Flowers are saucer-shaped, with white,
purplish, reddish, or greenish petals.
Berries are roundish, red, sticky, bristly,
to ⅜" across.

Leaves are deeply and palmately dissected into toothed, sticky, hairy lobes.

Grows on talus slopes and ridges, and
in forests and boulder fields.

Life Zones: Montane to Alpine

Flowering Time: June to August

Broom Huckleberry

(Red Billberry, Grouseberry, Red
 Whortleberry, Grouse Whortleberry)

Vaccinium scoparium
(V. erythrococcum)

Heath Family (Ericaceae)

Low shrub, to 10" high, with erect,
sharply angled, broomlike branches.

Flowers are single, with white or
pinkish corollas. Berries are bright
red and less than ¼" across.

Leaves are oval to elliptical, shiny,
and small (to ⅜" long).

Grows in conifer forests and on
grassy tundra.

Life Zones: Montane to Alpine

Flowering Time: June to August

Mountain Blueberry

(Blueberry, Myrtle Blueberry,
Myrtle Whortleberry)

*Vaccinium myrtillus
oreophilum*

Heath Family (Ericaceae)

Low shrub, to 18" high,
with spreading, sharply
angled branches.

Flowers are urn-shaped
and drooping, with white
to pinkish corollas. Berries
are ⅜" across and dark blue.

Leaves are about ¾" long,
oval, and smooth, with
small teeth.

Grows in rocky areas and
forest openings.

Life Zones:
Montane to Alpine

Flowering Time:
June to August

Red-Berried Elder

(Red Elderberry, Stinking Elder)

Sambucus microbotrys
(S. pubens, S. racemosa)

Honeysuckle Family (Caprifoliaceae)

Coarse shrub, to 10' tall, with warty bark.

Flowers are white, smelly, in pyramid-shaped clusters. Berries are ¼" wide, orange to red.

Leaves are opposite, pinnately compound, to 4¾" long, with 5 to 7 sharp-toothed leaflets.

Grows in moist sites in meadows, forest openings, ravines, and along streams.

Life Zones: Montane and Subalpine

Flowering Time: May to July

Mountain Ash

(Rowan Tree)

Sorbus scopulina

Rose Family (Rosaceae)

Small tree or tall shrub, to 15' high, in thickets, with smooth, grayish bark and shiny, reddish twigs.

Flowers are small, white, in 6" clusters; berries are about 5/16" wide and bright red.

Leaves are alternate, compound, to 5" long; leaflets (usually 11) are up to 2" long, dark green on top and grayish below, with toothed margins.

Prefers cool, moist places, such as ravines, canyons, and stream banks.

Life Zones:
Foothills to Subalpine

Flowering Time: May to July

Mountain Spray
(Rock Spirea, Creambush,
 Ocean Spray)
Holodiscus dumosus

Rose Family (Rosaceae)

Shrub, to 8' tall, much-branched, with gray, shredded branchlets and dark red twigs.

Flowers are tiny, pinkish white, in conical clusters to 8" long.

Leaves to 2" long, silky beneath, with toothed margins.

Common on rocky slopes and canyon walls, and among outcrops and cliffs.

Life Zones:
Foothills and Montane

Flowering Time: June to August

Mountain Dryad

(White Dryad, Alpine Avens,
Mountain Avens, White Alpine
Avens, Alpine Rose)

Dryas octopetala

Rose Family (Rosaceae)

Dwarf shrub, to 8" tall, with
creeping, mat-forming stems.

Flowers are 1" across, with 8
broad, white petals and 8 sticky,
hairy, pointed sepals. The styles
become silky plumes at maturity.

Leaves are elliptical, to 1½" long,
leathery, and shiny, with lobed
margins and white, hairy lower
surfaces.

Grows in tundra and on exposed
ridges and slopes.

Life Zone: Alpine

Flowering Time: July and August

Ninebark
(Colorado Ninebark, Rocky
 Mountain Ninebark)

Physocarpus monogynus

Rose Family (Rosaceae)

Shrub, to 6' high, with arching
stems that shed bark in layers;
upper branchlets are red.

Flowers are white, in small
clusters; fruit is tiny and greenish
to reddish brown.

Leaves are palmately lobed into
three to five segments that are
toothed and turn bright red in
the fall.

Common on rocky slopes and in
ravines, aspen groves, and forest
openings.

Life Zones: Foothills to Subalpine

Flowering Time: June and July

Pin Cherry

(Bird Cherry, Wild Red Cherry)

Prunus pensylvanica

Rose Family (Rosaceae)

Shrub or small tree to 12'
tall, with smooth, brown bark
split by lenticels.

Flowers are saucer-shaped,
with white petals, in a loose
cluster; cherries are small (to
⅜" in diameter), smooth,
and bright red.

Leaves are oval, to 3" long,
bright green above and pale
below, with finely toothed
margins.

Grows in canyons and ravines
and along streams.

Life Zones:
Foothills and Montane

Flowering Time: May and June

Thimbleberry
(Salmonberry, White-Flowering Raspberry)

Rubacer parviflorum

Rose Family (Rosaceae)

Shrub, to 6' tall, with shredding, grayish bark and bright green branchlets; forms large, dense patches.

Flowers are large (to 1½" across), white, and papery; berries are red, to ¾" wide, and edible.

Leaves are very large (to 8" across) and palmately lobed into 3 or 5 toothed segments, dark green above, and bluish green below.

Common in cool, damp areas, such as ravines, canyons, streamsides, and forest openings.

Life Zones: Foothills to Subalpine

Flowering Time: May and June

Engelmann Aster

(White Aster)

Eucephalus engelmannii
(Aster engelmannii)

Aster Family (Asteraceae)

Perennial, to 5' high, with erect, stout, leafy stems. Grows in clumps from rootstocks.

Flower heads are large (to 2½" across), in clusters. Ray flowers (to 15) are white or faintly pinkish and twisted; disk is yellow; bracts are tiered, broad, with papery margins.

Leaves are lance-shaped, to 4" long, and pale and hairy beneath.

Grows in wet areas on stream banks and pond shores, and in forest openings.

Life Zones: Montane and Subalpine

Flowering Time: July to September

Porter Aster

Aster porteri

Aster Family (Asteraceae)

Perennial, to 18" high, in tufts, with wiry stems.

Flower heads are small (¾" across) and numerous. Ray flowers are white; the disk is dark yellow; bracts are reflexed and 3-tiered.

Leaves are narrow, to 4" long, and bright green.

Grows in fields, meadows, and forest openings, along roads, and on hillsides.

Life Zones:
Foothills to Subalpine

Flowering Time:

July to October

Blackheaded Daisy

Erigeron melanocephalus

Aster Family (Asteraceae)

Perennial, to 5" tall, with twisted, slightly hairy stem.

Flower heads are single, to 1½" across, with white to pinkish ray flowers, yellow disks, and woolly, blackish bracts.

Leaves to 1½" long; basal leaves are stalked and spoon-shaped.

Common on tundra slopes, in meadows, and along forest edges.

Life Zones: Subalpine and Alpine

Flowering Time: July and August

Coulter Daisy

Erigeron coulteri

Aster Family (Asteraceae)

Perennial, to 2' tall, with slender rootstock and erect, hairy, leafy stems.

Flower heads are single, to 1½" across, with up to 100 white or pale lavender rays. Bracts have long, blackish hairs.

Leaves are broadly oblong and hairy, with the lower leaves stalked and toothed.

Prefers moist areas on stream banks and in meadows, forest openings, and aspen groves.

Life Zones: Foothills to Subalpine

Flowering Time: June to August

Cutleaf Daisy

(Cutleaf Fleabane, Cutleaf Erigeron,
 Dwarf Mountain Fleabane, Gold Buttons)

Erigeron compositus

Aster Family (Asteraceae)

Perennial, to 8" tall, in clumps, with creeping rootstock and short, stout stems.

Flower heads are single, to 1" across, with many white to pinkish ray flowers and yellow, buttonlike disks.

Leaves are mostly basal and dissected 4 times into linear segments that are 3-lobed and sticky.

Prefers dry areas, such as rocky slopes, moraines, forest openings, and fields.

Life Zones: Foothills to Subalpine

Flowering Time: April to August

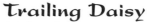

Trailing Daisy
(Trailing Fleabane, Running Fleabane, Whiplash Daisy)

Erigeron flagellaris

Aster Family (Asteraceae)

Biennial, to 16" tall, with runners and slender, twisted stem.

Flower heads are small (to ¾" in diameter) and single. Ray flowers (as many as 100 per head) are white on top and tinged bluish or pinkish beneath; disk is yellow and greenish; bracts are pointed, sticky, and hairy.

Leaves are mostly basal, to 1½" long, green, and soft, with rough margins.

Common in exposed sites, such as hillsides, meadows, and prairies, and along ditches.

Life Zones: Plains to Subalpine

Flowering Time: April to August

Frosty Ball

(Alpine Thistle, Woolly Thistle)

Cirsium scopulorum
(C. hookerianum)

Aster Family (Asteraceae)

Perennial, to 2' tall, with stout, erect, spiny stem.

Flower heads (to 5) are in dense, nodding clusters; flowers are creamy white to yellow, but are hidden by white, cobwebby hairs and spiny bracts.

Leaves are lance-shaped, to 6" long, thick, and deeply incised; teeth are tipped by ½" long spines.

Common along roads and trails, and on rocky or gravelly slopes.

Life Zones:
Subalpine and Alpine

Flowering Time:
July to September

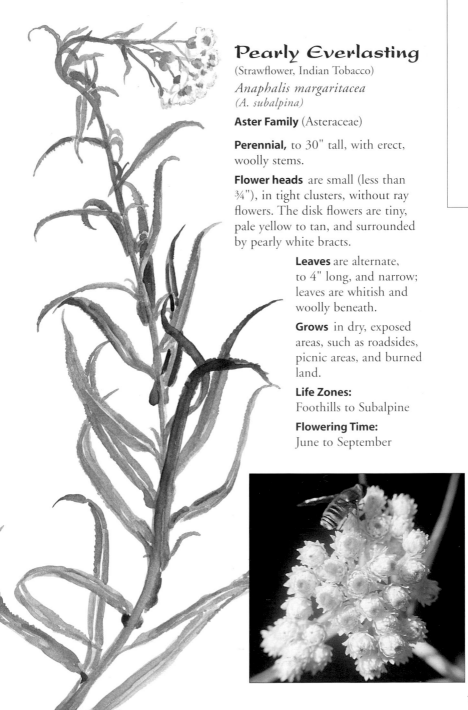

Pearly Everlasting

(Strawflower, Indian Tobacco)

Anaphalis margaritacea
(A. subalpina)

Aster Family (Asteraceae)

Perennial, to 30" tall, with erect, woolly stems.

Flower heads are small (less than ¾"), in tight clusters, without ray flowers. The disk flowers are tiny, pale yellow to tan, and surrounded by pearly white bracts.

Leaves are alternate, to 4" long, and narrow; leaves are whitish and woolly beneath.

Grows in dry, exposed areas, such as roadsides, picnic areas, and burned land.

Life Zones:
Foothills to Subalpine

Flowering Time:
June to September

Alpine Pussytoes

(Alpine Catspaw)

Antennaria umbrinella
(A. alpina)

Aster Family (Asteraceae)

Perennial, to 4" tall, with short, slender runners forming mats, and erect, leafy, woolly stems.

Flower heads are in clusters, on short stalks, with brown bracts; male and female heads are on separate plants.

Leaves are basal, spatulate with pointed tips, to 1" long, whitish and hairy beneath.

Common in forest openings and meadows, and on slopes.

Life Zones: Montane to Alpine

Flowering Time: July and August

Rosy Pussytoes

Antennaria microphylla
(A. arida, A. bracteosa, A. viscidula)

Aster Family (Asteraceae)

Perennial, to 12" tall, densely hairy; forms mats via runners.

Flower heads are small, without ray flowers; the white disk and papery, tan to pink bracts provide color.

Leaves are small (less than ¾" long), spatulate, and hairy.

Common on hillsides and prairies, and in meadows and open woods.

Life Zones: Plains to Subalpine

Flowering Time: May to August

Tall Pussytoes

Antennaria pulcherrima
anaphaloides
(A. anaphaloides)

Aster Family (Asteraceae)

Perennial, to 16" tall (much shorter at high elevations), with hairy, silvery stems.

Flower heads are small, in clusters of up to 20, with woolly, white or tannish bracts.

Leaves are narrowly lance-shaped, hairy on both sides, with parallel veins.

Found in open areas, such as gravelly and sandy hillsides, dry meadows, aspen groves, and forest clearings.

Life Zones: Foothills to Subalpine

Flowering Time: June to August

Sunloving Catspaw
(Small-Leaved Pussytoes, Nuttall's Pussytoes,
 Mountain Pussytoes)

Antennaria parvifolia
(A. aprica)

Aster Family (Asteraceae)

Perennial, to 6" tall, mat-forming,
 and densely woolly.

Flower heads to ½" across, without
ray flowers; papery bracts are white
with pinkish tips.

Leaves to 1" long, spatulate, and
woolly.

Abundant on dry, sunny hillsides
and wooded slopes, and in forest
openings.

Life Zones: Foothills to Subalpine

Flowering Time: June to September

Tasselflower

(Thoroughwort, Sheathflower,
Brickellbush)

Brickellia grandiflora
(Coleosanthus grandiflorus,
C. umbellatus)

Aster Family (Asteraceae)

Perennial, to 28" tall,
with erect, branched,
leafy stem.

Flower heads to 2" high,
in clusters, without ray
flowers; the disk flowers are
creamy white, sometimes
yellowish or greenish.

Leaves are alternate, heart-
shaped, to 5" long, smooth
on top, and hairy beneath.

Common in dry, chalky
soils on cliffs, rocky slopes,
and canyon sides.

Life Zones:
Foothills and Montane

Flowering Time:
July to October

American Thistle

(Weakspine Thistle)

Cirsium centaureae
(C. americanum, Carduus americanus,
C. centaurea)

Aster Family (Asteraceae)

Perennial, to 3' tall, in colonies, with erect, reddish, cobwebby stems.

Flower heads to 1½" high, without ray flowers. Disk flowers are white to tannish, with purple stripes; bracts are spine-tipped, with latticelike hairs.

Leaves are deeply incised, whitish and hairy beneath, and spiny.

Commonly found in ravines and forest openings, and on rocky slopes and banks.

Life Zones:
Montane and Subalpine

Flowering Time: June to August

Colorado Thistle

(Elk Thistle, Drummond's Thistle,
 Everet's Thistle)

Cirsium coloradense
(C. drummondii, C. oreophilum,
 Carduus drummondii)

Aster Family (Asteraceae)

Perennial, to 4' tall, usually
with stout, green to reddish
stems, although stemless plants
occur.

Flower heads are large (to 2"
across), in clusters, with creamy
white to purplish disk flowers and
short, hairy bracts. There are no
ray flowers.

Leaves are alternate, to 14" long,
light green above, and silvery
beneath, with spiny teeth.

Prefers moist areas, such as
meadows, ditches, stream banks,
and aspen groves.

Life Zones: Montane and Subalpine

Flowering Time: June to August

Creamy Thistle

Cirsium canescens

Aster Family (Asteraceae)

Perennial, to 3' tall, with stout, branched, cobwebby stem.

Flower heads to 1¼" high, with creamy white disk flowers and no ray flowers.

Leaves to 8" long, bright green on top and whitish beneath, extending down the stem, with spines of varying lengths on the margins.

Common on slopes, in clearings, fields, and meadows, and along roads.

Life Zones: Foothills and Montane

Flowering Time: July to September

Alpine Yarrow
Achillea alpicola

Aster Family (Asteraceae)

Perennial, to 10" tall, with erect, tough, hairy, reddish stem.

Flower heads are in umbel-like cluster, with roundish, white ray flowers (⅛" wide, usually 5 per head), yellow or tannish disk flowers, and hairy bracts with dark brown margins.

Leaves are narrow, tail-like, to 4" long, and dissected into featherlike leaflets.

Grows in exposed areas along roads and trails, in forest openings, and on tundra slopes.

Life Zones:
Subalpine and Alpine

Flowering Time:
July to September

Tansy Yarrow

(Yarrow, Milfoil)
Achillea lanulosa

Aster Family (Asteraceae)

Perennial, to 3' tall, aromatic, with erect, slender stem.

Flower heads are in flat-topped, umbel-like clusters, with small, white to pinkish ray flowers, yellow disk flowers, and hairy bracts.

Leaves are narrow, to 5" long, and pinnately dissected into narrow leaflets.

Grows in dry areas along roads and trails, in clearings, and on hillsides and slopes.

Life Zones: Foothills to Alpine

Flowering Time: May to September

Wild Chamomile

Matricaria perforata
(M. inodora, M. maritima,
Chamomilla inodora, C. maritima)

Aster Family (Asteraceae)

Annual, to 2' tall, with several stems, branched near top.

Flower heads to 2" across. Ray flowers (about 20) are white; disks are yellow and mound-shaped; bracts are green and brown.

Leaves are alternate, about 2" long, and finely dissected into linear, fleshy leaflets.

Common in disturbed areas along roadsides, around buildings, and in pastures and fields.

Life Zones:
Montane and Subalpine

Flowering Time:
July to October

Globeflower

(White Globeflower, American Globeflower)

Trollius albiflorus
(T. laxus albiflorus, T. laxus)

Buttercup Family (Ranunculaceae)

Perennial, in clumps, to 18" tall, with hairless, stout stem.

Flowers are saucer-shaped, to 1½" across. The petal-like sepals are white to creamy (turning brown later), roundish, and prominently veined; the small, yellowish petals surround the many stamens and pistils.

Leaves are deeply dissected into 5 or 7 lobes with large teeth.

Common in wet areas around springs, near snow banks, along streams and lake shores, and in meadows and forest openings.

Life Zones: Montane to Alpine

Flowering Time: May to August

Marsh Marigold

(White Marsh Marigold, Mountain
Marsh Marigold, Cow's Lip,
Elk's Lip, Meadowbright)

Psychrophila leptosepala
(Caltha leptosepala)

Buttercup Family
(Ranunculaceae)

Perennial, to 8" tall, with erect,
leafless flower stalks.

Flowers are bowl-shaped, to 1½"
across, without petals. Flowers have
many stamens and pistils that form
a yellow center, surrounded by
about 10 petal-like sepals that are
white with bluish veins.

Leaves are basal, to 3" long,
heart-shaped, thick, dark green,
and short-stalked.

Grows in large patches in bogs,
marshes, and soggy meadows, along
lakes and ponds, and at the edges
of snowfields.

Life Zones: Subalpine and Alpine

Flowering Time: June to September

Thimbleweed

(Candle Anemone)

Anemone cylindrica

Buttercup Family (Ranunculaceae)

Perennial, to 2' tall, with slender, silky stems.

Flowers are about ¾" across, cup-shaped, with up to 9 white tepals. The seed head is cylindrical, to ¾" high, and woolly.

Leaves are large, long-stalked, fan-shaped, and deeply dissected.

Found in ditches and meadows, and along roads.

Life Zones:
Plains to Montane

Flowering Time:
May and June

Caraway

Carum carvi

Celery Family (Apiaceae)

Biennial, to 3' tall, with erect, smooth stem and curved, twisted branches.

Flowers are tiny (less than ¼" wide), white, and clustered in small umbels that form the main umbel.

Leaves are pinnately dissected 3 times into linear leaflets.

Grows in disturbed areas, such as neglected fields, roadsides, and pastures.

Life Zones:
Foothills and Montane

Flowering TIme:
May to July

Cowbane

(Hogfennel)

Oxypolis fendleri

Celery Family (Apiaceae)

Perennial, to 3' tall, with weak, round, hollow stem.

Flowers are tiny (about ¹⁄₁₆" wide), in small umbels to 2½" wide, with 5 roundish, white petals.

Leaves are pinnately divided into 7 to 9 ovate leaflets that are soft and have blunt teeth.

Grows in wet spots in meadows and bogs, along streams, and near springs.

Life Zones:
Montane and Subalpine

Flowering Time:
June to August

Cow Parsnip

(Bear's Breeches, Cow Cabbage,
Hogweed, Masterwort, Hercules
Parsnip)

*Heracleum sphondylium
montanum*
*(H. lanatum, H. maximum,
H. sphondylium)*

Celery Family (Apiaceae)

Perennial, to 8' high, in patches,
with stout, hairy stem.

Flowers are small and grouped
into umbels that form larger (to
12" wide), flat-topped umbels.
The 5 petals are white, oval, and
sweet-smelling.

Leaves are divided into 3 coarse-
toothed leaflets; lower leaflets are
larger than the other two (to 16"
across).

Common in wet areas, such as
stream banks, willow thickets,
bogs, swamps, aspen groves, and
meadows.

Life Zones: Foothills to Subalpine

Flowering Time: May to August

Giant Angelica

Angelica ampla

Celery Family (Apiaceae)

Perennial, to 7' tall, with coarse, stout, purplish stems.

Flowers are tiny, many, and white (turning greenish or brownish); flowers form small umbels (about 1" across) that make up the large main umbel.

Leaves are large and divided twice into toothed leaflets.

Grows in shady, wet places, such as meadows, woods openings, and stream banks.

Life Zones:
Foothills and Montane

Flowering Time:
July and August

Lovage

(Loveroot, Porter Lovage,
 Osha, Wild Celery, Wild Parsnip)

Ligusticum porteri
(L. affine, L. simulans)

Celery Family (Apiaceae)

Perennial, to 3½' tall, with stout, hollow, reddish, smelly stem.

Flowers are small (less than ¼" wide), with white to pinkish petals; the flowers are clustered into flat-topped umbels that form the main umbel.

Leaves are fernlike, to 10" long, ending in 3" long leaflets.

Common in meadows, woods, forest ravines and openings, and aspen groves.

Life Zones: Foothills to Subalpine

Flowering Time: July and August

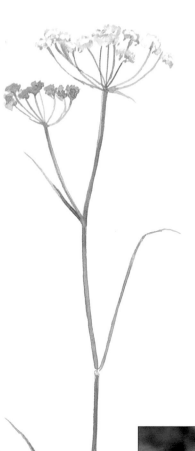

Yampa
(Squawroot, Wild Caraway,
False Caraway)

Perideridia gairdneri borealis

Celery Family (Apiaceae)

Perennial, to 3' tall, with erect, wiry, smooth stem.

Flowers are tiny, with white, scoop-shaped petals and green, hemispherical calyx; flowers are in small, stalked umbels that make up the primary umbel.

Leaves are split into threadlike leaflets to 6" long.

Grows in moist places in western Colorado, such as aspen groves, slopes, and valley floors.

Life Zones:
Foothills and Montane

Flowering Time:
July and August

Field Mouse Ear

(Mouse-Ear Chickweed, Field Chickweed,
 Meadow Chickweed, Mouse-Ear)

Cerastium strictum
(C. arvense)

Chickweed Family (Alsinaceae)

Perennial, to 10" tall, with weak
but erect stems, in large patches.

Flowers are small (less than ½"
across), in loose clusters, with
white, deeply cleft petals.

Leaves are opposite, about 1"
long, linear, sticky, and hairy.

Grows in dry areas, chalky soil on
hillsides, gravelly slopes, prairies,
and in pastures and forest openings.

Life Zones: Plains to Alpine

Flowering Time: February to August

Starwort

(Chickweed, Longstalk Starwort)

Stellaria longipes
(S. laeta, S. monantha, Alsine longipes,
A. laeta, A. monantha, A. stricta)

Chickweed Family (Alsinaceae)

Perennial, to 8" tall, with angular, slender, erect stem.

Flowers are single and terminal, ½" across, with 5 white, deeply cleft petals and 5 green and white sepals.

Leaves are opposite, to 1½" long, shiny, and firm.

Grows in moist areas, such as stream banks, seepage depressions, pond shores, and mossy hummocks.

Life Zones: Foothills to Alpine

Flowering Time: May to August

James Starwort

Pseudostellaria jamesiana
(Stellaria jamesiana)

Chickweed Family (Alsinaceae)

Perennial, to 8" tall, spidery, with fragile stem and threadlike branches that are angular.

Flowers are star-shaped, on long stalks at the tips of branches; the 5 petals are white and deeply cleft.

Leaves are opposite, to 3" long, pointed, and narrow.

Common but often overlooked in thickets, forest openings, meadows, and on slopes.

Life Zones:
Foothills and Montane

Flowering Time: July and August

Umbrella Starwort

Stellaria umbellata
(S. weberi, Alsine baicalensis)

Chickweed Family (Alsinaceae)

Perennial, to 16" tall in the shade and just 2" in the sun, with spidery, weak branches.

Flowers are less than ⅛" long, with no petals and papery, white sepals that have green keels.

Leaves are small (about 1" long), opposite, slender, and pointed.

Common in moist, shady areas in ravines and gullies, along streams, and in thickets and forests.

Life Zones:
Subalpine and Alpine

Flowering Time:
June to August

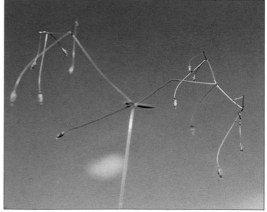

Baby's Breath

(Groundsmoke)

Gayophytum diffusum parviflorum

Evening Primrose Family (Onagraceae)

Annual or biennial, to 12" high, profusely and intricately branched, with slender, shiny stem and branches.

Flowers are tiny (¹⁄₁₆" long), with 4 roundish, white to reddish petals and 4 reflexed, slender sepals. The seed pod is stringlike, to ¾" long, with ¼" stalks.

Leaves are slender, to 1" long; lower leaves are stalked.

Grows in sand and gravel along roads and on hillsides.

Life Zones: Montane and Subalpine

Flowering Time: July and August

Alpine Willowweed

(Alpine Willowherb)

Epilobium alpinum
(E. anagallidifolium, E. hornemannii)

Evening Primrose Family (Onagraceae)

Perennial, to 16" tall, in tufts, with runners and slender stem.

Flowers are tiny; the 4 petals are ³⁄₁₆" long, notched, and white to pinkish, and the sepals are about ⅛" long. The seed capsules are long, slender, hairy, to 2¾" long.

Leaves are oval, thin, to ¾" long, and blunt.

Found in wet environments, such as low meadows, tundra pools, stream banks, and snowmelt rivulets.

Life Zones: Montane to Alpine

Flowering Time: June to September

Milky-Flowered Willowherb

(White Epilobium)

Epilobium lactiflorum

Evening Primrose Family
(Onagraceae)

Perennial, to 12" high, in bunches, with erect, smooth stems.

Flower is a 1" long tube, with 4 white, pink-tipped petals at the end. The seed capsule is long (to 2") and slender.

Leaves are opposite, to 2" long, and toothed.

Grows on moist ground in meadows and along streams and forest brooks.

Life Zones:
Montane and Subalpine

Flowering Time:
June to September

Parry Lousewort

Pedicularis parryi

Figwort Family (Scrophulariaceae)

Perennial, to 16" tall, with many erect, smooth stems.

Flowers are 2-lipped, to ¾" across, in a spike, and white to yellowish or pinkish; the flower's upper lip is sickle-shaped, curving downward, with a short beak; the ½" calyx is dark-veined.

Leaves are mostly basal, to 4¾" long, and pinnately divided into narrow, toothed lobes.

Grows in dry meadows and on talus slopes and hillsides.

Life Zones: Subalpine and Alpine

Flowering Time: July and August

Sickletop Lousewort

(Mountain Figwort, Curled Lousewort,
 Leafy Lousewort, Parrot's Beak, Ram's Horn)

Pedicularis racemosa alba

Figwort Family (Scrophulariaceae)

Perennial, in clumps, to 2' tall,
with angular, reddish stems.

Flowers are in terminal racemes,
with 2-lipped, creamy white corolla.
The upper lip is twisted downward
into a sicklelike beak, and the lower
lip is 3-lobed and spreading.

Leaves are narrow, to 3½" long, often
reddish, with small, sharp teeth.

Common along trails, on slopes,
and in conifer woods.

Life Zones: Montane and Subalpine

Flowering Time: July and August

Snowlover
Chionophila jamesii

Figwort Family
(Scrophulariaceae)

Perennial, to 4" tall, with fleshy, erect to leaning stem.

Flowers are in a one-sided cluster (to 8 flowers per cluster), with a tubular, white, ¾" long corolla and greenish white calyx.

Leaves are fleshy, 1½" long, and spatulate. Basal leaves have broad stalks; stem leaves are stalkless and smaller.

Found in wet tundra and near rivulets, snow banks, and streams.

Life Zone: Alpine

Flowering Time:
July and August

Arctic Gentian

Gentianodes algida
(Gentiana romanzovii)

Gentian Family (Gentianaceae)

Perennial, in clumps, to 6" high, with short stem.

Flowers (to 3 per stem) are barrel-shaped, to 2" long, white to greenish, with purplish streaks on the outside and spots inside; the pistil is green and club-shaped, and the anthers are reddish.

Leaves are narrowly oblong, to 3" long.

Found in grassy areas along stream banks, in meadows, and near ponds.

Life Zones:
Subalpine and Alpine

Flowering Time: August

Green Gentian

(Monument Plant, Deer's Ears, Elkweed)

Frasera speciosa
(Swertia radiata)

Gentian Family (Gentianaceae)

Biennial, to 6' tall, with stout, erect, unbranched stem.

Flowers are many, clustered along the stem, with 4 or 5 slender sepals. The 4 or 5 petals are greenish white, joined at the base, with purple glands and stiff hairs on the inside.

Leaves are narrowly lance-shaped, to 18" long, whorled, and pale green.

Prefers chalky soil in fields and meadows, along roadsides, and on grassy slopes.

Life Zones:
Foothills to Subalpine

Flowering Time:
June to August

White Geranium

(Richardson's Geranium,
 Richardson's Cranesbill)

Geranium richardsonii
(G. gracilentum)

Geranium Family (Geraniaceae)

Perennial, to 3' high, with slender,
weak stems.

Flowers are in pairs, 1" wide, with
5 white petals that have pink veins,
and 5 long-tipped, sharp sepals.
Flowers are on long, sticky stalks.

Leaves to 6" across, on long stalks,
deeply cleft into 5 to 7 pointed lobes.

Grows in moist, shaded locations,
such as aspen groves, forests, meadows,
and road banks.

Life Zones:
Foothills to Subalpine

Flowering Time:
May to August

Wood Nymph

(Shy Maiden, Single Delight,
Waxflower, One-Flowered
Wintergreen, Star-Flowered Pyrola)

Moneses uniflora
(Pyrola uniflora)

Heath Family (Ericaceae)

Perennial, delicate, to 5" high, with fleshy stem.

Flower is single, saucer-shaped, 1" wide, nodding, and very fragrant. The 5 petals are white (rarely pinkish), waxy, and fused at the base; the 5 sepals are tiny, with bristly margins. The ovary is large, bulbous, and 5-lobed.

Leaves (as many as 8) are in a basal rosette, evergreen, to 1" long.

This shy, little beauty grows in dark forests, in moss mounds, and near springs and streams.

Life Zones: Montane and Subalpine

Flowering Time: June to August

Bistort

(American Bistort, Western Bistort,
 Smartweed, Knotweed, Snakeweed)

Bistorta bistortoides
(Polygonum bistortoides)

Knotweed Family (Polygonaceae)

Perennial, to 2' tall, with erect,
slender stem and twisted root.

Flowers are white to pinkish,
to ³⁄₁₆" long, with no petals but
5 petal-like sepals; flowers are in
a dense, cylindric raceme.

Leaves to 10" long, narrow, with
papery sheaths.

Very common in tundra, on slopes
and hillsides, and in meadows.

Life Zones: Subalpine and Alpine

Flowering Time: June to August

Serpentgrass

Bistorta vivipara

Knotweed Family (Polygonaceae)

Perennial, to 12" tall, with slender, erect stem.

Flowers are white to pinkish, in a spikelike cluster; dark bulblets occupy lower part of the cluster.

Leaves to 4" long, alternate, slender, with inrolled margins.

Grows in exposed areas, such as meadows, tundra slopes, and hillsides.

Life Zones: Subalpine and Alpine

Flowering Time: June to August

Alpine Lily

(Alplily)

Lloydia serotina

Lily Family (Liliaceae)

Perennial, to 6" tall, with bulblike rootstock.

Flowers to ¾", drooping, with 3 sepals and 3 petals that are alike, white with greenish bases and purplish veins.

Leaves are grasslike, to 6" long.

This beauty hides in rock crevices, on cliffs, among boulders, and in meadows.

Life Zone: Alpine

Flowering Time: June and July

Death Camas

(Wand Lily, Poison Camas, Poison Sego, Alkali Grass, White Camas, Mountain Death Camas)

Anticlea elegans
(Zigadenus elegans)

Lily Family (Liliaceae)

Perennial, to 20" high, with several erect stalks.

Flowers are saucerlike, to ¾" wide, in racemes, with 6 white tepals (petals and sepals are undifferentiated).

Leaves are basal, linear, and smooth, with parallel veins.

Grows in moist areas along streams and in forest clearings and meadows. *Poisonous.*

Life Zones: Foothills to Alpine

Flowering Time: June to August

Cornhusk Lily

(False Hellebore, False White Hellebore,
 Corn Lily, California Corn Lily, Skunk
 Cabbage)

Veratrum tenuipetalum
(V. californicum, V. speciosum)

Lily Family (Liliaceae)

Perennial, to 7' tall, in dense patches,
with stout, leafy stem.

Flowers are small, with 6 white
to greenish tepals (undifferentiated
petals and sepals), in long clusters.
Berries are red.

Leaves are large (to 12" by 8"), with
prominent parallel veins and pleated
margins.

Grows mostly west of the Continental
Divide, in moist, low places, such as
meadows, river and creek bottoms,
bogs and swamps, and mossy forest
openings. *Poisonous.*

Life Zones: Montane and Subalpine

Flowering Time: June to August

Mariposa Lily

(Star Tulip)

Calochortus gunnisonii

Lily Family (Liliaceae)

Perennial, grows from bulb, to 20" tall, with slender stem, in patches.

Flowers are cup-shaped, to 2" across, with white petals and three translucent, whitish or pale green sepals.

Leaves are narrow, to 10" long.

Common in meadows and open woods, and on slopes.

Life Zones: Foothills to Subalpine

Flowering Time: May to July

Northern Bedstraw

(Cleavers, Bedstraw)

Galium septentrionale
(G. boreale)

Madder Family (Rubiaceae)

Perennial, to 2½' tall, with shiny, flexible, angular stems.

Flowers are ⅛" across, in small clusters, with 4 white petals; the sepals are missing.

Leaves are many, whorled, 4 per node, to 2" long, and dark green on top.

Found mostly along roads, in open woods and meadows, and on slopes.

Life Zones: Plains to Subalpine

Flowering Time: May to August

Star Solomon's Seal

(Star Flower, Star Solomon Plume, False
Solomon's Seal, Wild Lily-of-the-Valley)

Maianthemum stellatum
(Smilacina stellata, Vagnera leptopetala,
V. stellata, V. liliacea)

Mayflower Family (Convallariaceae)

Perennial, to 2' high, in patches, with
erect, leafy stem.

Flowers are in 2" long clusters, with
3 petals and 3 sepals; both are white.
Berries are reddish to purplish black.

Leaves are alternate, to 6" long,
and pointed.

Grows in moist woods and open
meadows, along streams, and on
gravelly shores.

Life Zones: Foothills to Subalpine

Flowering Time: April to July

Bitter Cress

(Brook Cress,
 Heartleaved Bitter Cress)

Cardamine cordifolia
(C. infausta)

Mustard Family (Brassicaceae)

Perennial, to 30" tall, in large patches, with tuberous rootstock and several upright, leafy stems.

Flowers are ¾" long, in a raceme; with 4 white, indented petals. The seed pods are flat and slender.

Leaves are heart-shaped and scalloped.

Grows in wet areas, such as stream banks, meadows, and forest depressions.

Life Zones:
Montane and Subalpine

Flowering Time: June to August

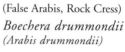

Drummond Rock Cress

(False Arabis, Rock Cress)

Boechera drummondii
(Arabis drummondii)

Mustard Family (Brassicaceae)

Perennial, to 3' tall, with slender, erect stems.

Flowers are small, with 4 white or pinkish petals. Seed pods are flat, to 4" long, and erect.

Leaves are mostly basal, to 3½" long, stalked, and fleshy.

Common on gravelly and rocky slopes, in meadows and forest openings, and along roads.

Life Zones:
Montane and Subalpine

Flowering Time: May to July

Mountain Candytuft

(Wild Candytuft, Mountain Pennycress)

Noccaea montana
(Thlaspi montana, T. alpestre,
  T. coloradense, T. fendleri, T. glaucum,
  T. nuttallii, T. purpurescens)

Mustard Family (Brassicaceae)

Perennial, to 10" tall, in clumps, with leafy stems.

Flowers are in short racemes; the 4 petals are white to purplish, spoon-shaped, and ¼" long; the 4 sepals are pointed, green and white with purplish tinges. Seed pod is erect, heart-shaped, winged, to ¼" long.

Leaves on stem are alternate and clasping; basal leaves are stalked and spoon-shaped.

Grows on hillsides and slopes, in open woods and forests, and on tundra.

Life Zones: Foothills to Alpine

Flowering Time: April to July

White Bog Orchid

(Scent Bottle, Bog Rein Orchid, Bog Candle)

Limnorchis dilatata albiflora
(Habenaria dilatata, H. dilatata albiflora)

Orchid Family (Orchidaceae)

Perennial, in bunches, with tuberous roots and sturdy, leafy stem.

Flowers are white and waxy, very fragrant, about ½" long, in spikes. Two petals and an oval sepal join to form a hood; the third petal is a drooping lip with a spur and expanded (dilated) base; the two other sepals are spread out.

Leaves are slender, to 8" long, alternate, and clasping.

Grows in wet areas, such as marshes, bogs, stream banks, damp woods, and pond shores.

Life Zones: Montane to Alpine

Flowering Time: June to September

Alpine Clover

(Whiproot Clover)

Trifolium dasyphyllum

Pea Family (Fabaceae)

Perennial, to 5" tall, in clumps forming mats, with slender, leafless, arched stems.

Flowers are in ball-like clusters, 2-lipped, white, with pinkish or purplish tips and white, slender, hairy sepals. The flower cluster is subtended by spinelike, green and white bracts.

Leaves are basal, long-stalked, and divided into 3 narrow, pointed, 1" long leaflets that are hairy beneath.

Common in tundra and on rocky or gravelly slopes.

Life Zones: Subalpine and Alpine

Flowering Time: June to August

Common Lupine

(Silvery Lupine)

Lupinus argenteus

Pea Family (Fabaceae)

Perennial, to 30" tall, with slender, hairy stem.

Flowers are in dense, spikelike clusters, 2-lipped, creamy white and bluish or pinkish. The seed pod is hairy, to 1" long.

Leaves are alternate and palmately divided into 7 to 11 slender leaflets that are silvery and hairy beneath, 2½" long.

Common in dry, open sites, such as fields and prairies, roadsides, forest openings, and hillsides.

Life Zones: Foothills to Subalpine

Flowering Time: June to September

White Loco

(Rocky Mountain Loco, Silverleaf Loco, Silky
Loco, Silky Crazyweed, White Point Loco)

Oxytropis sericea
(C. saximontana)

Pea Family (Fabaceae)

Perennial, to 16" tall, in large colonies,
with curved, silky, grayish stems.

Flowers are numerous, white, to 1" long,
in dense clusters, with purple-tipped
keel and silky sepals that have black tips.

Leaves are pinnately compound, to
12" long, with silky, silvery leaflets
(up to 21). Seed pods are erect, plump,
to 1" long.

Grows in gravelly areas of open fields,
prairies, mountain meadows, and slopes.

Life Zones: Plains to Subalpine

Flowering Time: May to August

White Peavine

(White Sweet Pea)

Lathyrus leucanthus
(L. laetivirens, L. arizonicus)

Pea Family (Fabaceae)

Perennial, in large patches, with vinelike stem.

Flowers are white (or creamy tannish), to 1" long, in few-flowered clusters.

Leaves are pinnately compound, with tendrils at tips and as many as 10 leaflets that reach 3" in length.

Grows in gulches and canyons, on hillsides, and in forest openings.

Life Zones: Plains to Subalpine

Flowering Time: May to July

Alpine Phlox

Phlox condensata

Phlox Family (Polemoniaceae)

Perennial, forming cushions, with 1" high stems and woody taproot.

Flowers are single, ¼" across, fragrant, with 5 white, roundish petals and sticky, hairy calyx lobes.

Leaves are fleshy, mosslike, to ³⁄₁₆" long.

Common on gravelly slopes, among boulders, and on rocky tundra.

Life Zone: Alpine

Flowering Time: June to August

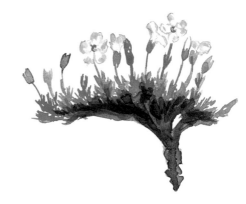

White Fairy Trumpet
(White Skyrocket)

Ipomopsis candida

Phlox Family (Polemoniaceae)

Biennial, to 3' tall, with slender, downy, sticky stem.

Flowers are showy, to 2" long, in long, one-sided panicle; corolla is trumpet-shaped, with white, spreading lobes.

Leaves are alternate, sticky, and finely divided into stringlike segments that are up to 2" long.

Thrives in exposed, sunny areas in pine woods and along roads and trails, especially on south-facing slopes.

Life Zones:
Foothills and Montane

Flowering Time: June to August

Alpine Mouse Ear

(Alpine Chickweed, Mountain
Chickweed)

Cerastium beeringianum earlei

Pink Family (Caryophyllaceae)

Perennial, to 8" high, with sticky,
erect to trailing stems, forming
mats.

Flowers are stalked, with 5 white,
deeply cleft petals and 5 sticky,
hairy sepals.

Leaves are opposite, to 1" long,
oblong, and hairy.

Common on tundra slopes and
ridges, in meadows, and on rocky
or gravelly hillsides.

Life Zone: Alpine

Flowering Time: June to August

Bladder Campion

(Maiden's Tears)

Silene vulgaris
(S. cucubalus)

Pink Family (Caryophyllaceae)

Perennial, to 2½' tall, with light green, stiff stem and decumbent, grooved, flower-bearing branches.

Flowers are loosely clustered, with inflated calyx and 5 white, notched petals.

Leaves to 3" long, opposite, lance-shaped, and hairless.

Common in dry meadows, pastures, and along roadsides.

Life Zones: Foothills and Montane

Flowering Time: June to September

Sandwort

(Fendler Sandwort)
Eremogone fendleri
(Arenaria fendleri)

Pink Family (Caryophyllaceae)

Perennial, to 10" tall, in clumps, with woody root and erect, slender, bluish stem.

Flowers (several) are in an open cluster, with 5 white petals and 5 papery, pointed sepals.

Leaves are grasslike, stiff, to 3" long.

Grows in sunny, dry areas, such as grassy slopes, hillsides, open woods, and clearings.

Life Zones: Foothills to Alpine

Flowering Time:
July to September

Alpine Sandwort

(Sandywinks)

Lidia obtusiloba
(Arenaria obtusiloba, Minuartia obtusiloba)

Pink Family (Caryophyllaceae)

Perennial, mat-forming, to 2" tall, with slender, fuzzy stems that are woody at the bases.

Flowers are single, ⅜" wide, with 5 white petals that have broad, indented tips, and 5 fuzzy, brown-tipped sepals.

Leaves are mosslike, ¼" long, sheathed in pairs.

Grows in sandy, disturbed areas on talus slopes and rocky tundra.

Life Zone: Alpine

Flowering Time: June to September

Alpine Rockjasmine

(Rock Jasmine)

Androsace chamaejasma carinata
(A. carinata, A. lehmanniana)

Primrose Family (Primulaceae)

Perennial, to 3" high, cushion-form-ing, with creeping, rooting, reddish, hairy stems.

Flowers are in roundish clusters (up to 6 per cluster) on short stalks, with 5 white, waxy, roundish petals and a bristly, cuplike calyx.

Leaves form basal rosette, to ⅜" long, fleshy, with hairy, bristly margins.

Common in tundra, on gravelly and rocky slopes, and among rock crevices.

Life Zone: Alpine

Flowering Time: June and July

Northern Rockjasmine

(Rock Primrose, Northern Androsace, Fairy Candelabra, Alpine Skyrocket)

Androsace septentrionalis

Primrose Family (Primulaceae)

Annual, to 8" tall, with smooth, wiry stems and long, slender flower stalks.

Flowers are tiny (to ¼"), in umbels subtended by bracts. Flowers have 5 roundish, white petals and 5 calyx lobes that are keeled, green, white, and reddish.

Leaves are in basal rosette, lance-shaped to spoon-shaped, to 1" long, with teeth near the tip.

Common in open areas, such as meadows, disturbed ground, tundra, and forest openings.

Life Zones: Foothills to Alpine

Flowering Time: May to August

Rock Primrose

(Northern Androsace)

Androsace septentrionalis subumbellata

Primrose Family (Primulaceae)

Annual, cushion-forming, to 6" tall, with wiry, smooth stems.

Flowers are ¼" wide, long-stalked, tubular, in loose umbels, with 5 white, roundish petals and 5 green and red sepals.

Leaves to 1" long, in basal rosette, sticky, and toothed.

Common in exposed areas, such as meadows, slopes disturbed by gophers or moles, and forest openings.

Life Zones: Foothills to Alpine

Flowering Time: May to August

Alpine Springbeauty

(Big-Rooted Springbeauty)

Claytonia megarhiza

Purslane Family (Portulacaceae)

Perennial, with stout taproot, forming round patches, to 5" high.

Flowers to ¾" across, with white, red-veined petals.

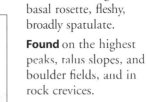

Leaves are in tight, basal rosette, fleshy, broadly spatulate.

Found on the highest peaks, talus slopes, and boulder fields, and in rock crevices.

Life Zone: Alpine

Flowering Time: June to August

Wild Strawberry

Fragaria virginiana glauca
(F. americana, F. ovalis, F. glauca,
F. pausiflora, F. prolifica)

Rose Family (Rosaceae)

Perennial, to 4" high, with long, red runners and hairy stems.

Flowers are saucer-shaped, to 1" across, in clusters, and on long, hairy stalks. The 5 roundish petals are white, and the 5 sepals are hairy and reflexed. Berries are red and delicious.

Leaves are divided into 3 leaflets about 1½" long, bluish green beneath, with hairy veins and coarse-toothed margins.

Grows in grassy meadows, moist woods and thickets, on slopes, and along forest borders.

Life Zones: Foothills to Subalpine

Flowering Time: April to August

Woodland Strawberry

(Wild Strawberry, European Wild Strawberry,
Earth Mulberry, Snowteat)

Fragaria vesca bracteata
(F. americana, F. bracteata, F. crinita)

Rose Family (Rosaceae)

Perennial, to 8" high, with long runners and slender, hairy stems and stalks.

Flowers are ¾" across, in clusters, with 5 roundish, white petals and 5 hairy sepals. Berries are juicy, red, and tasteless.

Leaves are basal and divided into 3 leaflets that are grayish and hairy beneath, to 2" long, and sharply toothed.

Grows near the borders of woods, in openings, thickets, and meadows, and on open hillsides.

Life Zones: Foothills to Subalpine

Flowering Time: April to September

Bog Saxifrage

(Alpine Bog Saxifrage)

Micranthes oregana
(Saxifraga oregana)

Saxifrage Family (Saxifragaceae)

Perennial, to 12" tall, with erect, stout, sticky, and densely hairy stem.

Flowers to ½" across, in stalked clusters that form a narrow raceme, with 5 white, oval petals and 5 reflexed, pointed sepals. The fruit is pear-shaped and reddish purple.

Leaves are basal, to 8" long, stalked, spoon-shaped, fleshy, and bright green, with reddish margins and small teeth.

Grows in wet environments, such as meadows, lake shores, stream banks, and willow thickets.

Life Zones: Subalpine and Alpine

Flowering Time: June to August

Brook Saxifrage

Micranthes odontoloma
(Saxifraga odontoloma, S. arguta)

Saxifrage Family (Saxifragaceae)

Perennial, to 20" tall, with naked, slender, sticky stem.

Flowers in a loose panicle, with 5 white petals, 5 red sepals, and 5 flat, white stamens with red anthers.

Leaves are basal, long-stalked, with 2" long, smooth, toothed blades.

Grows in wet areas of meadows and near waterfalls, streams, springs, and seepage areas.

Life Zones: Montane to Alpine

Flowering Time:
July to September

Nodding Saxifrage

Saxifraga cernua

Saxifrage Family (Saxifragaceae)

Perennial, to 7" tall, with erect, twisted, sticky stem.

Flowers to ⅝" across, with 5 white petals and a cup-shaped, hairy calyx. Red, budlike bulblets are clustered in the leaf axils.

Leaves are palmately lobed, stalked, and sticky.

Grows in moist areas along meltwater rivulets and near springs and seeps.

Life Zone: Alpine

Flowering Time: June to August

Snowball Saxifrage

(Diamondleaf Saxifrage,
Early Saxifrage)

Micranthes rhomboidea
(Saxifraga rhomboidea)

Saxifrage Family (Saxifragaceae)

Perennial, to 12" tall, with leafless, erect, sticky stem.

Flowers are cup-like, have 5 white petals, 5 green sepals, and form ball-like clusters.

Leaves are basal, to 3" long, thick, and smooth, with broad, short stalks and blunt teeth.

Grows in open areas disturbed by gophers and moles, in meadows, and on rocky slopes.

Life Zones: Foothills to Alpine

Flowering Time: May to August

Spotted Saxifrage

(Dotted Saxifrage)

Ciliaria austromontana
(Saxifraga bronchialis)

Saxifrage Family (Saxifragaceae)

Perennial, to 6" tall, mat-forming, with slender, sticky, reddish stem.

Flowers to ⅜" across, in open panicle, with 5 white petals dotted purplish red, 5 maroon sepals, and 10 white, protruding stamens.

Leaves are mostly basal, tightly stacked, mosslike, and rigid, with spiny tips and bristly margins.

Grows in dry areas along trails, on rocky slopes, and in forest openings and boulder fields.

Life Zones: Foothills to Alpine

Flowering Time: June to August

Snow Alumroot

Heuchera parvifolia nivalis

Saxifrage Family (Saxifragaceae)

Perennial, in clumps, to 9" tall, with wiry, twisted, sticky stem.

Flowers are in short-stalked clusters that form a narrow panicle, with ¼", white to yellowish petals and bristly sepals.

Leaves are in basal rosette, long-stalked, palmately lobed, with bristly, red margins.

Grows on rocky or gravelly slopes and hillsides.

Life Zones: Subalpine and Alpine

Flowering Time: June to August

Tall Valerian

(Edible Valerian, Tobacco Root)

Valeriana edulis

Valerian Family
(Valerianaceae)

Perennial, to 2' tall, with fleshy taproot and smooth, erect stem.

Flowers are small and white, in stalked clusters that form an open panicle with opposite branching.

Leaves are large (to 6" long), fleshy, narrow, and velvety beneath.

Grows in wet areas on tundra, meadows, and slopes.

Life Zones:
Montane to Alpine

Flowering Time:
July and August

Western Valerian

Valeriana occidentalis
(V. micrantha)

Valerian Family (Valerianaceae)

Annual, to 28" tall, with creeping rootstock and erect, curving, grooved stem.

Flowers are tiny and clustered in panicles that are compact when young, open and loose when mature. The corolla is white or yellowish, and the calyx develops into a parachutelike tuft of bristles.

Leaves at the base are entire, spatula-shaped, and stalked; leaves on the stem are opposite, stalkless, and pinnately lobed.

Common in wet places, such as meadows, bogs, seepage slopes, stream banks, and pond shores.

Life Zones: Foothills to Subalpine

Flowering Time: July to September

Lesser Wintergreen

(Least Wintergreen)

Pyrola minor
(Erxlebenia minor)

Wintergreen Family (Pyrolaceae)

Perennial, to 8" tall, with runners and erect, angular, leafless stems.

Flowers are small, round, in raceme. The 5 petals are white to pinkish, and the calyx is pale green and papery.

Leaves are basal, to 1½" long, roundish, leathery, and smooth.

Found in moist, shady places, such as boggy thickets, seepage pools, stream banks, moss hummocks, and dark forests.

Life Zones: Montane and Subalpine

Flowering Time: June to August

One-Sided Wintergreen

(Sidebells, Sidebells Wintergreen,
 One-Sided Pyrola)

Orthilia secunda
(Pyrola secunda, Ramischia secunda)

Wintergreen Family (Pyrolaceae)

Perennial, to 8" high, in patches, with branching rootstock and upright stem.

Flowers are small (to ¼" long) and nodding, in one-sided raceme. The 5 petals are greenish white and fleshy, and the 5 sepals are papery.

Leaves are deep green, persistent through winter, leathery, shiny, oval to roundish, to 2½" long.

Prefers cool, moist, shady spots in willow thickets and forests, on mossy hummocks, along streams, and beside springs.

Life Zones: Foothills to Subalpine

Flowering Time: June to August

Mountain Sage

Seriphidium vaseyanum
(Artemisia tridentata vaseyana)

Aster Family (Asteraceae)

Shrub, to 3' tall, with peeling, brown and tan bark and slender, whitish to tannish twigs.

Flower heads are ¼" high, in narrow panicles, with silvery green, densely hairy bracts and tannish yellow flowers.

Leaves are 1½" long, in whorls, wedge-shaped, bluish to silvery green, densely hairy, with 3 pointed lobes at the tip.

Grows on dry hillsides and rocky slopes, and in mountain parks, aspen groves, and forest openings.

Life Zones: Montane and Subalpine

Flowering Time: July to September

Dwarf Rabbitbrush

(Sticky-Flowered Rabbitbrush)

Chrysothamnus viscidiflorus

Aster Family (Asteraceae)

Low shrub, creeping, much-branched from base, with shaggy bark. Satiny twigs, to 10" high, bear the flower heads.

Flower heads are small, slender, and many, in flat-topped clusters. There are no ray flowers; the 5 disk flowers are golden yellow and 5-lobed; the bracts (about 15) are green, in 3 tiers.

Leaves are alternate, stalkless, narrow, to 2¼" long, and twisted.

Common in western Colorado on dry hillsides and in deserts and open woods.

Life Zones: Foothills to Subalpine

Flowering Time:
July to September

Mountain Rabbitbrush

Chrysothamnus parryi affinis

Aster Family (Asteraceae)

Low shrub, creeping, much-branched at base, with 12" high, shiny twigs.

Flower heads are narrow, to ½" long, in terminal and axillary clusters, with no ray flowers and only a few (to 10) pale yellow, satiny disk flowers sticking out of the leafy, slender bracts.

Leaves are narrow, tapered at both ends, to 3" long, leathery, and fuzzy.

Grows on sagebrush slopes and in dry forest openings in western Colorado.

Life Zones: Foothills to Subalpine

Flowering Time: July to September

Hollygrape
(Oregon Grape, Creeping Hollygrape,
 Creeping Mahonia, Mountain Holly)

Mahonia repens
(Berberis repens)

Barberry Family (Berberidaceae)

Shrub, to 10" high, creeping,
with underground stems; forms
large patches.

Flowers are small and in clusters.
Berries are oval, juicy, and dark blue.

Leaves are pinnately
compound, with
evergreen, spiny, 3"
long leaflets.

Common on hill-
sides and in conifer
woods and scrub
oak thickets.

Life Zones:
Foothills and
Montane

Flowering Time:
April to June

Mountain Mahogany

(Featherbush)

Cercocarpus montanus

Rose Family (Rosaceae)

Shrub, to 8' high, with erect, grayish brown stem and stiff branches.

Flowers are inconspicuous, to ¼" long, and tubular, with no petals; the calyx lobes are yellowish and red-tipped. Fruit has 4" long, hairy, twisted tail.

Leaves are dark green on top and pale beneath, with toothed margins and prominent veins.

Common in dry areas, such as exposed slopes and rocky hillsides.

Life Zones: Foothills and Montane

Flowering Time: June and July

Shrubby Cinquefoil

(Yellow Rose, Bushy Cinquefoil)

Pentaphylloides floribunda
(Potentilla floribunda, P. fruticosa,
Dasiophora fruticosa)

Rose Family (Rosaceae)

Shrub, to 3' tall, with much-branched stem and shredding bark.

Flowers are clustered, to 1½" wide, with 5 rounded, bright yellow petals and 5 hairy, papery sepals.

Leaves are pinnately divided into 3 to 7 leaflets that are grayish, hairy, leathery, and less than 1" long.

Prefers moist ground in meadows and depressions, along pond shores, and on ridges.

Life Zones: Foothills to Alpine

Flowering Time: June to September

Broadleaf Arnica
Arnica latifolia

Aster Family (Asteraceae)

Perennial, to 10" high, with slender, sticky stem.

Flower heads to 1½" across, to 3 per stem, with about 9 bright yellow ray flowers and many dark yellow disk flowers. Bracts are long (to ½"), green and white, hairy, and pointed.

Leaves to 2" by 1", oval to triangular, opposite, with winged stalks and sharply toothed margins.

Found in moist, shady forests.

Life Zone: Subalpine

Flowering Time: June and July

Heart-Leaved Arnica

(Leopard's Bane)

Arnica cordifolia

Aster Family (Asteraceae)

Perennial, to 2' tall, with single, velvety stem.

Flower heads are large (to 3" across), with about 10 bright yellow ray flowers, many dark yellow disk flowers, and hairy bracts.

Leaves are opposite, stalked, to 4" long, velvety, and heart-shaped.

Common in moist, shaded sites, such as thickets and woods.

Life Zones: Foothills to Subalpine

Flowering Time: June to August

Rayless Arnica

(Parry Arnica, Nodding Arnica)

Arnica parryi

Aster Family (Asteraceae)

Perennial, to 20" tall, with slender rootstock and hairy, wiry stem.

Flower heads are bell-shaped, to ¾" high, with no ray flowers. Disk flowers are dark yellow, and the bracts are short and purple-keeled.

Leaves are opposite, with up to 4 pairs on the stem. Basal leaves are larger, stalked, and lance-shaped, with hairy mid-veins and margins.

Grows in moist meadows, parks, open forests, and aspen groves.

Life Zones: Montane to Alpine

Flowering Time: July and August

Subalpine Arnica
(Hairy Arnica, Tall Subalpine Arnica)

Arnica mollis
(A. coloradensis, A. subplumosa,
A. silvatica)

Aster Family (Asteraceae)

Perennial, to 2' tall, with sticky, hairy, stems.

Flower heads are large (2" across), with bright yellow, indented ray flowers, hemispherical disks, and pointed bracts.

Leaves are opposite, soft, hairy, and sticky, with short teeth on the margins.

Grows in moist forest soil and near streams, springs, and melting snow banks.

Life Zones: Subalpine and Alpine

Flowering Time: June to August

Golden Aster

(Goldaster)

Heterotheca fulcrata

Aster Family (Asteraceae)

Perennial, in clumps, to 2' tall, with slender, rough, reddish stems.

Flower heads to 1¼" across, in loose, leafy clusters. Ray flowers are yellow and slender; the disk is yellow to orange; bracts are slender, brown-tipped, and hairy.

Leaves are grayish, hairy, to 1½" long, with bristly margins.

Common on sunny slopes and hillsides, and in meadows and forest clearings.

Life Zones:
Montane and Subalpine

Flowering Time:
July to September

Dwarf Golden Aster

(Golden Aster)

Heterotheca pumila

Aster Family (Asteraceae)

Perennial, to 5" high, grows in circular mounds from one root, with many woody, reddish, woolly stems.

Flower heads to 1¼" across, with bright yellow ray flowers, ⅜" wide orange disk, and hairy, green and white bracts.

Leaves are crowded near top of the stem, about 1½" long, with sticky stalks and spoon-shaped blades; lower leaves wither early.

Grows on tundra and avalanche slopes, in boulder fields, and along roads and trails.

Life Zones: Subalpine and Alpine

Flowering Time: July and August

Blackeyed Susan

(Browneyed Susan)

Rudbeckia hirta

Aster Family (Asteraceae)

Perennial, to 30" tall, with erect, purple-tinged, rough, hairy stem.

Flower heads to 3" across, with dome-shaped (to ¾" high), blackish brown disks, orange to yellow ray flowers with toothed tips, and fleshy, bristly bracts.

Leaves are simple, alternate, to 6" long, and hairy.

Common in aspen groves, open woods, and meadows, on hillsides, and along trails and roads.

Life Zones: Foothills and Montane

Flowering Time: July and August

164

Blanketflower

(Gaillardia, Perennial Gaillardia, Brown-Eyed Susan)

Gaillardia aristata

Aster Family (Asteraceae)

Perennial, to 28" tall, with several erect, hairy stems.

Flower heads are large (to 3½" across), with brown to maroon disks, yellow to reddish ray flowers, and bristly, sharply pointed bracts.

Leaves to 4" long, lance-shaped, rough, and hairy.

Grows in open, sunny areas, such as hillsides, meadows, and clearings in woods.

Life Zones: Plains to Montane

Flowering Time: June to August

165

Cutleaf Agoseris

(Pale Agoseris, False Dandelion)

Agoseris glauca laciniata
(A. laciniata)

Aster Family (Asteraceae)

Perennial, less than 8" tall, with erect, leafless, hairy stalk and milky sap.

Flower heads are pale yellow, to 1" across, with no disk flowers; bracts are narrow and hairy. The one-seeded fruit is tufted, with a long beak.

Leaves are basal, to 5" long, and coarsely toothed.

Grows on slopes, in meadows and forest openings, and along trails.

Life Zones: Foothills to Subalpine

Flowering Time: June to August

False Dandelion

Microseris nutans

Aster Family (Asteraceae)

Perennial, to 2' tall, with slender, grooved stem.

Flower heads are small, to ¾" across, with light yellow, indented ray flowers. Disk flowers are dark yellow; the bracts are woolly and slender.

Leaves are mostly basal, to 4" long, slender, and fleshy, with large teeth.

Grows in open woods and dry meadows, and on hillsides.

Life Zones: Montane and Subalpine

Flowering Time: July to September

Tall False Dandelion

(Hairy False Dandelion, Mountain
Dandelion, Pale Agoseris, Goat Chicory)

Agoseris glauca dasycephala
(Troximon glaucum)

Aster Family (Asteraceae)

Perennial, to 2' tall, with erect,
leafless, woolly stalk and milky sap.

Flower heads are large (to 2" across),
pale yellow, with no disk flowers;
bracts are black-haired. Fruit is one-
seeded, tufted, and with a short, stout
beak.

Leaves are basal, to 14" long and
¾" wide, entire to slightly lobed.

Common on hillsides and sage slopes,
and in meadows and forest openings.

Life Zones: Foothills to Alpine

Flowering Time: May to September

Tundra Dandelion

(Horned Dandelion)

Taraxacum ovinum
(T. ceratophorum, T. dumetorum,
T. leiospermum, T. montanum)

Aster Family (Asteraceae)

Perennial, to 10" high, with smooth, hollow, leafless stem.

Flower heads are single, large (to 2" across), with no disk flowers; the ray flowers are golden yellow, and the bracts have hornlike tips.

Leaves are basal, in a rosette, firm, and shallow-toothed.

Grows in meadows and on tundra slopes and ridges.

Life Zone: Alpine

Flowering Time: June to August

Goldeneye

(Sunspots)

Heliomeris multiflora
(Viguiera multiflora,
Gymnoloma multiflora)

Aster Family (Asteraceae)

Perennial, to 3' tall, with several slender, wiry, rough stems.

Flower heads are 1¾" across, with conical, yellow to orange disks and broad, golden yellow ray flowers.

Leaves are narrow, to 4" long, tapered, and bristly.

Common in dry areas, such as hillsides, clearings in woods, and along roadsides.

Life Zones:
Foothills and Montane

Flowering Time:
August and September

Alpine Goldenrod

(Mountain Goldenrod)

Solidago multiradiata scopulorum

Aster Family (Asteraceae)

Perennial, in clumps, to 20" tall, with reddish, erect stem.

Flower heads are small, in a narrow panicle, with about 12 ray flowers, many yellow disk flowers, and many slender bracts in 3 tiers.

Leaves are mostly basal, to 4" long, stalked, fleshy, smooth, spatulate, and pointed.

Grows in sunny, exposed areas on grassy slopes, along ridges, and among boulders.

Life Zones: Subalpine and Alpine

Flowering Time: July to September

Dwarf Goldenrod

Solidago spathulata nana
(S. decumbens, S. oreophila)

Aster Family (Asteraceae)

Perennial, to 10" tall, with erect or leaning, reddish stem.

Flower heads are small (⅜" high), in compact clusters, with about 8 golden yellow ray flowers and a few more disk flowers; bracts are green and white, linear.

Leaves are spatulate, to 2½" long, soft, smooth, and stalked, with toothed tips.

Grows in sunny, exposed areas, such as slopes, ridges, talus, and boulder fields.

Life Zones: Subalpine and Alpine

Flowering Time: July to September

Smooth Goldenrod

(Missouri Goldenrod,
 Tight Goldenrod)

Solidago missouriensis
(S. concinna)

Aster Family (Asteraceae)

Perennial, to 18" high, with hairless stems; grows in clumps via runners.

Flower heads are very small, in clusters to 8" long. Both ray flowers and disk flowers are yellow; bracts are blunt and green.

Leaves are ascending, smooth, to 5" long, leathery, with bristly margins.

Common on rocky slopes, stream banks, and roadsides, and in ditches and forest openings.

Life Zones:
Plains to Montane

Flowering Time:
July to September

Alpine Goldenweed

(Alpine Tonestus, Lyall's Goldenweed)

Tonestus lyallii
(Haplopappus lyallii)

Aster Family (Asteraceae)

Perennial, to 6" tall, with branched rootstock and several slender, erect stems.

Flower heads are single, to 1" across, with yellow ray flowers and pointed, sticky, overlapping bracts.

Leaves are spatulate, to 2¾" long, sticky, and alternate.

Grows in rocky tundra, on ridges, and among boulders.

Life Zone: Alpine

Flowering Time: July to September

Pygmy Goldenweed

(Dwarf Goldenweed, Pygmy Tonestus)

Tonestus pygmaeus
(Haplopappus pygmaeus)

Aster Family (Asteraceae)

Perennial, to 2½" tall, forming cushions, with woody root and hairy stems.

Flower heads are single, large (¾" wide), with reflexed, golden yellow, indented ray flowers and bristly, hairy, grayish bracts.

Leaves are spatulate, to 1½" long, thick, folded, grayish, and hairy, with bristly margins.

Grows in gravelly, rocky areas, such as talus slopes, boulder fields, ridges, and tundra.

Life Zone: Alpine

Flowering Time: July and August

Alpine Groundsel

(Daffodil Senecio)

Ligularia amplectens
(Senecio amplectens)

Aster Family (Asteraceae)

Perennial, to 2' tall, with smooth, erect stem.

Flower heads to 3" across and nodding. Ray flowers are pale yellow, separate, and spreading; disk is dark yellow and dome-shaped; bracts are ¾" long, purplish.

Leaves are large (to 8" long), smooth, toothed, and sessile; lower leaves wither early.

Common in forest clearings and rocky areas, such as talus slopes and boulder fields.

Life Zones: Subalpine and Alpine

Flowering Time:
July to September

Fendler Groundsel
(Fendler's Senecio)

Packera fendleri
(Senecio fendleri)

Aster Family (Asteraceae)

Perennial, to 18" tall, with slender stem.

Flower heads to ¾" wide, in clusters. Ray flowers are bright yellow, clawed, with indented tips; disks are large and yellow; bracts are slender, pointed, with white margins.

Leaves are narrow, to 3½" long, alternate, and comblike.

Common in dry areas, such as rocky and gravelly slopes, hillsides, and forest openings.

Life Zones: Foothills to Alpine

Flowering Time: May to August

Lambstongue Groundsel

(Common Spring Senecio,
 Early Spring Senecio)

Senecio integerrimus
(S. perplexus)

Aster Family (Asteraceae)

Perennial, to 2' tall, with stout, hollow, grayish, cobwebby stem.

Flower heads are small (less than ¾" across), in crowded clusters. Ray flowers are bright yellow; disks are tannish yellow; bracts are black-tipped and brown-veined.

Leaves to 6" long, cobwebby, and grayish.

Prefers dry sites along roads, on hillsides and sloping meadows, and in forest openings.

Life Zones: Foothills to Subalpine

Flowering Time: April to July

Rock Groundsel

(Hoary Ragwort)

Packera werneriifolia

Aster Family (Asteraceae)

Perennial, to 8" tall, in clumps, with erect, woolly, reddish stems.

Flower heads have orange disks, golden yellow ray flowers with indented tips, and tiered, woolly, reddish green bracts.

Leaves are basal, 2" long, thick, narrow, and woolly beneath.

Grows in gravelly and rocky areas, such as tundra slopes, boulder fields, outcrops, and ridges.

Life Zones: Subalpine and Alpine

Flowering Time: June to September

Saffron Groundsel

(Saffron Senecio, Orange Ragwort)

Packera crocata
(Senecio crocata)

Aster Family (Asteraceae)

Perennial, to 2' tall, with single, stout, grooved, hairless stem.

Flower heads to 1½" across, in tight cluster. Ray flowers are clawed and spoon-shaped, with indented tips; the disk is dark orange; bracts are woolly, to ½" long, black-tipped with white margins.

Leaves are thick, fleshy, and lobed. The upper leaves are smaller and clasping, and the basal leaves are stalked, to 3" long.

Grows in moist areas, such as bogs, marshes, meadows, and stream banks.

Life Zones: Montane to Alpine

Flowering Time: June to September

Woolly Groundsel

(Pursh Senecio)

Packera cana
(Senecio cana, S. harbourii, S. purshiana)

Aster Family (Asteraceae)

Perennial, to 8" high, in patches, with leafy stems.

Flower heads are large, to 1½" across, with light yellow ray flowers, small, dark yellow disks, and slender, sharp, woolly bracts.

Leaves to 2" long, woolly, and spoon-shaped.

Prefers dry sites, such as moraines, boulder fields, gravelly and rocky tundra, rocky slopes, and hillsides.

Life Zones: Foothills to Alpine

Flowering Time: July and August

Mountain Gumweed

Grindelia subalpina

Aster Family
(Asteraceae)

Perennial, to 18"
tall, with tough,
flexible, much-
branched stem.

Flower heads are numerous,
to 1½" across, with bright
yellow ray flowers, small
yellow disks, and reddish,
reflexed, sticky bracts.

Leaves are alternate, to 3"
long, thick, and sharply
toothed.

Prefers dry areas and
disturbed soil along roads,
 in meadows, and on slopes.

Life Zones:
Montane and Subalpine

Flowering Time:
 July to September

Orange Sneezeweed

(Sneezeweed, Western Sneezeweed, Owl-Claws)

Dugaldia hoopesii
(Helenium hoopesii)

Aster Family (Asteraceae)

Perennial, to 4' tall, with stout, erect, leafy stem.

Flower heads several, large (to 3"), with yellow to orange, mound-shaped disks and drooping, narrow, yellow to orange ray flowers that have 3-toothed tips and are to 1½" long.

Leaves are alternate, thick, ovate to lanceolate; the lower leaves are stalked and to 10" long, the upper are reduced and sessile.

Common in southern and western Colorado; in aspen groves, open woods, meadows, and along roads. *Poisonous:* Causes "spewing sickness" in sheep.

Life Zones: Foothills to Subalpine

Flowering Time: June to September

Rock Ragwort

(Rock Senecio, Fremont's Groundsel)

Senecio fremontii blitoides
(S. cathamoides)

Aster Family (Asteraceae)

Perennial, to 12" high, with tough, leafy stems.

Flower heads to 1½" across, on curved stalks, with clawed, bright yellow ray flowers, dark yellow to orange disks, and reflexed outer bracts.

Leaves are oval, to 1½" long, thick, smooth, and coarsely toothed.

Grows in rocky areas, such as talus slopes, boulder fields, outcrops, and rock crevices.

Life Zones: Subalpine and Alpine

Flowering Time: July to September

Western Golden Ragwort

Senecio eremophilus kingii

Aster Family (Asteraceae)

Perennial, to 2½' tall, with leafy, ribbed stems.

Flower heads are less than ¾" across, in many clusters. The ray flowers are golden yellow and spaced apart, disks are dark yellow, and bracts are pointed, black-tipped, with white margins.

Leaves are alternate, to 4" long, smooth, and deeply and sharply toothed.

Common along roads and trails, and on hillsides and slopes.

Life Zones:
Foothills to Subalpine

Flowering Time:
July to September

Alpine Sage

(Rocky Mountain Sagewort, Dwarf Sage,
 Alpine Mountain Sage)

Artemisia scopulorum

Aster Family (Asteraceae)

Perennial, to 8" tall, with reddish,
hairy stem.

Flower heads are ³⁄₁₆" across, short-
stalked, nodding, in dense racemes.
Flower heads have no ray flowers;
the disk flowers are yellow (tinged
greenish and brownish), and the
bracts are hairy with purplish margins.

Leaves are mostly basal and twice-
dissected into narrow lobes that are
soft, hairy, and grayish.

Grows on tundra slopes, along trails,
and in disturbed areas and meadows.

Life Zones: Subalpine and Alpine

Flowering Time: July and August

Fringed Sage

(Silver Sage, Mountain Sage,
 Pasture Mountain Sage)

Artemisia frigida

Aster Family (Asteraceae)

Perennial, to 12" tall, in tufts, with erect, leafy, hairy stems.

Flower heads are tiny, in spikelike clusters, nodding, and yellow.

Leaves are in basal tufts and are deeply divided into silvery, ½" lobes.

Common on dry hillsides, and in meadows and clearings in woods.

Life Zones: Plains to Subalpine

Flowering Time:
July to October

Arrowleaf Senecio

(Triangleleaf Ragwort,
 Butterweed)

Senecio triangularis

Aster Family (Asteraceae)

Perennial, to 5' tall, in clumps, with stout, tough, leafy stems.

Flower heads to 1" wide, in clusters, with several bright yellow ray flowers, a small, yellow disk, and ½" long, brown-ribbed bracts.

Leaves are alternate, to 6" long, triangular, and coarsely toothed.

Common in moist areas in forests and meadows, near streams, and along pond shores.

Life Zone: Subalpine

Flowering Time:
June to September

Black-Tipped Senecio

Senecio atratus

Aster Family (Asteraceae)

Perennial, to 3½' tall, in clumps, with stout, ribbed, hairy stems.

Flower heads are small (½" wide), in many clusters. Ray flowers are bright yellow and spaced apart, disks are orange, and bracts are fuzzy, with black tips and white margins.

Leaves are large (to 12" long), alternate, soft, fleshy, and woolly, with toothed margins.

Common along roads and trails, and in scree and rock slides.

Life Zones: Montane and Subalpine

Flowering Time: June to August

Thick-Bracted Senecio

(Thick-Leaved Groundsel)

Senecio crassulus
(S. semiamplexicaulis, S. lepathifolius)

Aster Family (Asteraceae)

Perennial, to 20" tall, in clumps, with erect, smooth stems.

Flower heads are on long stalks, with golden yellow, slender, separated ray flowers, yellow-orange disk, and bulging, green, white, and brown bracts.

Leaves to 5" long (even stem leaves are large), fleshy, smooth, and finely toothed.

Grows in moist situations, such as stream banks, lake shores, and meadows.

Life Zones:
Subalpine and Alpine

Flowering Time:
June to August

Alpine Sunflower

(Old-Man-of-the-Mountain,
Mountain Sunflower, Alpine
Goldflower, Sun God, Rydbergia)

Rydbergia grandiflora
(Hymenoxys grandiflora)

Aster Family (Asteraceae)

Perennial, to 10" tall, with
stout, grayish, woolly stems.

Flower heads are very large
(to 4" across), single, and
nodding, with bright yellow,
notched ray flowers, a large,
domed disk, and narrow,
woolly bracts.

Leaves are mostly basal, to
4" long, and divided into
narrow, woolly, grayish lobes.

Grows on ridges and slopes,
among boulders, and in meadows.

Life Zone: Alpine

Flowering Time: July and August

Bush Sunflower

(Dwarf Sunflower, Perennial
Sunflower)

Helianthus pumilus

Aster Family (Asteraceae)

Perennial, to 30" tall, bushy,
with several rough and hairy
stems.

Flower heads are large (to
3⅛" across), with yellow or
tan disks and broad, yellow
ray flowers.

Leaves are opposite, short-
stalked, broadly lance-shaped,
and rough.

Grows in eastern
Colorado, in dry
areas such as open
woods, meadows,
slopes, hillsides,
and roadsides.

Life Zones:
Foothills and Montane

Flowering Time:
June to August

Nodding Sunflower

(Aspen Sunflower, Little Sunflower,
Five-Vein Sunflower, Five-Nerved Sunflower)

Helianthella quinquenervis

Aster Family (Asteraceae)

Perennial, to 4' tall, with several erect, leafy stems growing from a horizontal rootstock.

Flower heads to 4" across, stalked, and nodding, with as many as 20 yellow, 5-nerved ray flowers. The disk is dark yellow to brownish maroon, and the bracts are broadly lance-shaped, bristly, and pointed.

Leaves to 12" long, opposite, leathery, and pointed, with up to 5 veins.

Grows in open woods, aspen groves, and meadows, along forest edges, and on slopes.

Life Zones: Montane and Subalpine

Flowering Time: June to August

Tall Coneflower

(Cutleaf Coneflower, Golden Glow)

Rudbeckia ampla
(R. laciniata)

Aster Family (Asteraceae)

Perennial, to 6' tall, branched at base, with leafy, grooved stems.

Flower heads are large (to 5" wide). The ray flowers are slender, toothed, and dark yellow; disks are cone-shaped, to 1" high, and greenish brown; bracts are oblong, unequal, and reflexed.

Leaves are alternate and deeply cut into as many as 7 lobes.

Grows in moist areas, such as meadows, grassy slopes, aspen groves, fields, roadsides, and stream banks.

Life Zones: Foothills and Montane

Flowering Time: July to September

Tarragon

Oligosporus campestris caudatus
(Artemisia campestris caudata, A. caudata,
A. forwoodii)

Aster Family (Asteraceae)

Biennial, to 30" tall, with taproot
and reddish, flexible, leafy stem.
Grows in clumps.

Flower heads are many, small (to
⅛" wide), orange, yellow, or green,
in one-sided panicle; bracts form
saucer-shaped whorl, to ⅛" high.

Leaves to 3" long, divided into
fleshy, stringy segments.

Common in dry, open areas, such
as fields and meadows, grassy slopes,
and roadsides.

Life Zones: Plains to Montane

Flowering Time: July and August

Woolly Actinella

(Woolly Actinea, Stemless
Hymenoxys)

Tetraneuris brevifolia
*(T. acaulis caespitosa, T. lanigers,
Hymenoxys acaulis caespitosa)*

Aster Family (Asteraceae)

Perennial, to 5" tall, with thick
rootstock and twisted, woolly
stem.

Flower heads to 1¼" wide,
with bright yellow ray flowers
and slender, woolly bracts.

Leaves are basal, to 2" long,
woolly, and silvery.

Grows on dry hillsides, rocky
slopes, exposed ridges, and
tundra.

Life Zones: Subalpine to Alpine

Flowering Time: June to August

Heart-Leaved Buttercup

Ranunculus cardiophyllus

Buttercup Family (Ranunculaceae)

Perennial, to 12" tall, with fleshy, hairy, stout but weak stem.

Flowers are on long stalks, with 5 yellow petals and 5 hairy sepals; flowers are subtended by 4 hairy, leaflike bracts. Seed heads are cylindrical and less than ½" long.

Stem leaves are split into 5 linear lobes; basal leaves are fan- or heart-shaped and deeply cut into 3 lobes or merely shallowly lobed. Both types of basal leaves are long-stalked.

Usually found around springs, along streams and ponds, and in moist meadows.

Life Zones: Montane and Subalpine

Flowering Time: June to August

Homely Buttercup

(Ugly Buttercup, Unlovely Buttercup,
 Unattractive Buttercup)

Ranunculus inamoenus
(R. micropetalus)

Buttercup Family (Ranunculaceae)

Perennial, to 12" tall, with slender,
wiry, reddish stems.

Flowers are small, with or without
petals (yellow when present). Fruit
heads are slender, cylindrical, about
½" long, and cottony.

Stem leaves are deeply dissected
into narrow segments; basal leaves are
wedge-shaped and not deeply cut.

Grows in moist environments, such
as lake shores, stream banks, and
seepage slopes.

Life Zones: Montane and Subalpine

Flowering Time: July and August

Snow Buttercup

(Alpine Buttercup, Mountain Buttercup)

Ranunculus adoneus

Buttercup Family (Ranunculaceae)

Perennial, to 10" tall, with smooth stems, in clusters.

Flowers to 1½" across, with glossy, golden yellow, overlapping petals and hairy, purplish sepals.

Leaves are deeply dissected into 6 narrow lobes.

Grows in wet areas near and even under snow, by streams and springs, in meadows, and on tundra.

Life Zones: Subalpine and Alpine

Flowering Time: June to August

Subalpine Buttercup

(Alpine Buttercup)

Ranunculus eschscholtzii
(R. exinius, R. alpelophylus, R. ocreatus)

Buttercup Family (Ranunculaceae)

Perennial, to 10" tall, with smooth, clustered stems.

Flowers to 1½" across, with waxy, bright yellow, rounded petals, sepals that fall off early, and numerous greenish yellow stamens.

Leaves are deeply and palmately dissected into 6 lobes.

Grows in wet areas, such as low meadows, stream banks, melting snow, talus slopes, and forest floors.

Life Zones: Subalpine and Alpine

Flowering Time: June to August

Gray's Angelica
Angelica grayi
Celery Family (Apiaceae)

Perennial, to 2' tall, with stout, rough stem.

Flowers are tiny, mainly yellowish but also whitish, greenish, brownish, or purplish. Flowers are in small (to 2" across), round umbels that make up the large, main umbel.

Leaves are divided into toothed leaflets.

Found in moist areas in depressions, meadows, and valleys, and on slopes and scree.

Life Zones: Subalpine and Alpine

Flowering Time: June to August

Alpine Parsley

Oreoxis alpina
(Cymopteris alpinus)

Celery Family (Apiaceae)

Perennial, to 4" tall, forming mats, with taproot and slender, leafless, sticky stems.

Flowers are tiny, short-stalked, in umbel-like clusters to ¾" across, with 4 waxy, yellow to creamy white petals.

Leaves are dissected pinnately into fingerlike segments.

Common on tundra slopes, talus, and granitic ridges.

Life Zone: Alpine

Flowering Time: June to August

Indian Balsam

(Desert Parsley, Fernleaf Biscuitroot,
 Carrotleaf Lomatium)

Lomatium dissectum multifidum
(Leptotaenis multifida, L. eatoni)

Celery Family (Apiaceae)

Perennial, to 3' high, with large,
fleshy, aromatic taproot and clumps
of stems.

Flowers are very small, yellow (or
purplish), in small umbels less than
½" across that form the main umbel.

Leaves are divided 4 times into
thick, ½" long lobes.

Found in Western Colorado, in dry
areas among outcrops, on rocky
slopes, and projecting from cliffs.

Life Zones:
Foothills and Montane

Flowering Time:
May and June

Mountain Parsley

(Yellow Mountain Parsley, Wild Yellow
Parsley, Mountain Spring Parsley)

Pseudocymopteris montanus
(P. sylvaticus, P. tenuifolius, P. multifidus,
P. tidestromii, P. versicolor, P. purpureus)

Celery Family (Apiaceae)

Perennial, to 2' tall, with long taproot
and slender, erect stems.

Flowers are tiny (to ⅛" across), bright
yellow, in clusters that form flat-topped
umbels barely 2" across.

Leaves are basal and long-stalked, with
pinnately divided blades that are smooth
and dark green.

Common in aspen groves, forest clearings, and woods, but also in meadows
and on rocky slopes.

Life Zones: Foothills to Alpine

Flowering Time: June to August

Whiskbroom Parsley

(Mountain Parsley)

Harbouria trachypleura

Celery Family (Apiaceae)

Perennial, to 20" tall (blooms when only 2" high), with flexible, slender, grooved stems.

Flowers are tiny (to ⅛" across), yellow, in small clusters that form a 2" wide, long-stalked umbel.

Leaves are divided twice into 3-fingered, threadlike segments; leaves are broomlike and mostly basal.

Common east of the Continental Divide in dry meadows and open woods, and on sunny slopes.

Life Zones:
Foothills and Montane

Flowering Time:
May to July

Bracted Lousewort

(Fernleaf Lousewort, Towering
Lousewort, Red Helmet, Wood Betony)

Pedicularis bracteosa paysoniana
(P. grayi)

Figwort Family (Scrophulariaceae)

Perennial, to 3' tall, with several
coarse, hairy stems.

Flowers are in spikelike raceme,
2-lipped, yellow with reddish to
purplish streaks. Upper lip is
hoodlike; lower lip is 3-lobed.

Leaves are stalked and divided
into fernlike leaflets with toothed
margins.

Common in moist areas of forest
edges and clearings, thickets,
meadows, and rocky slopes.

Life Zone: Subalpine

Flowering Time: June to August

Alpine Paintbrush

Castilleja puberula
(C. flavoviridis, C. brachyantha)

Figwort Family (Scrophulariaceae)

Perennial, to 6" high, in clumps, with erect or leaning, hairy, woody stems.

Flowers are inconspicuous; the corolla is up to 1" long and greenish yellow, and the ½" calyx is cleft into 3 lobes that are greenish yellow and woolly.

Leaves are slender, yellowish green, and woolly; the lower leaves are entire, and the upper ones are lobed.

Grows on high ridges, tundra slopes, and steep hillsides.

Life Zones: Subalpine and Alpine

Flowering Time: July and August

Western Paintbrush

(Yellow Paintbrush, Western Yellow
 Paintbrush, Lemon Paintbrush)

Castilleja occidentalis

Figwort Family (Scrophulariaceae)

Perennial, to 12" tall, in clumps,
with woolly, unbranched stem.

Flowers are inconspicuous, greenish
yellow; the yellow, cleft bracts and
upper leaves provide the attraction.

Leaves are ascending, with slender
tips; upper leaves are cleft, and lower
leaves are entire.

Grows on peaks, in tundra and
forest openings, and on hillsides.

Life Zones: Subalpine and Alpine

Flowering Time: July to September

Yellow Paintbrush

(Northern Paintbrush, Sulphur Paintbrush, Squawfeather, Painted Cup)

Castilleja sulphurea
(C. brunnescens, C. luteovirens, C. septentrionalis)

Figwort Family (Scrophulariaceae)

Perennial, in clumps, to 20" tall, with erect, unbranched stems.

Flowers are tubular, to 1¼" long; the upper lip is yellow, long, and slender, and the lower lip is merely a green bump. The yellow (to whitish) color is provided by the bracts, not the flowers.

Leaves to 3" long, smooth, and lance-shaped; leaves hug the stem.

Grows in moist areas of meadows and foest glades, along stream banks, and near pools.

Life Zones: Plains to Subalpine

Flowering Time: May to September

Yellow Monkeyflower

(Common Monkeyflower, Common Yellow
Monkeyflower, Wild Lettuce)

Mimulus guttatus
(M. hallii, M. langsdorfii, M. puberulus)

Figwort Family (Scrophulariaceae)

Perennial, to 3' tall, with weak, hollow,
square stem that may be erect or reclining.

Flowers are tubular and 2-lipped; the
upper lip is 2-lobed, and the lower lip
is large and 3-lobed.

Leaves are opposite, to 3" long, oval,
with toothed margins.

Grows along streams and in seepages,
mossy areas, beaver dams, and ponds.

Life Zones: Foothills to Subalpine

Flowering Time: April to September

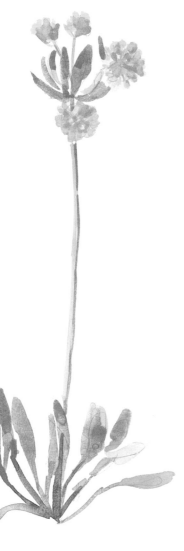

Sulphur Flower
Eriogonum umbellatum

Knotweed Family (Polygonaceae)

Perennial, mat-forming, to 16" tall, with leafless, felty stem.

Flowers are small (¼" long), bell-shaped, sulphur yellow, in clusters that form 4" umbels. Leaflike bracts subtend each umbel

Leaves are basal, in a rosette, stalked, and 2" long.

Common in dry forest openings and on rocky slopes and road banks.

Life Zones: Foothills to Subalpine

Flowering Time: June to August

Alpine Sulphur Flower

Eriogonum jamesii xanthum
(E. flavum, E. xanthum, E. crassifolium)

Knotweed Family (Polygonaceae)

Perennial, to 3" tall, with stout, hairy stem and woody root.

Flowers are tiny (to ¼"), golden yellow, in a tight cluster, with protruding stamens and styles.

Leaves are basal, grayish, woolly, 1" long, with rounded tips.

Found in gravelly, rocky areas, such as tundra slopes and ridges.

Life Zone: Alpine

Flowering Time: July and August

Winged Buckwheat

(Winged Eriogonum, Tall Yellow Eriogonum)

Pterogonum alatum
(Eriogonum alatum)

Knotweed Family (Polygonaceae)

Perennial, to 3½' tall, with woody taproot and erect, hairy stem. It requires several seasons to flower.

Flowers are small, greenish yellow, in small clusters that form a loose panicle. The fruit is roundish, flat, bristly, ⅜" long, with a rimlike wing.

Leaves are basal, in rosette, to 8" long and ½" wide, with pinkish, winged stalks and scattered hairs on top.

Common on mesas and hillsides, in parks, and at the edges of thickets.

Life Zones:
Foothills and Montane

Flowering Time:
June to August

Avalanche Lily

(Snow Lily, Glacier Lily, Dogtooth Violet,
 Fawn Lily, Adder's Tongue)

Erythronium grandiflorum

Lily Family (Liliaceae)

Perennial, in large patches, to 12"
tall, with erect, smooth, slender stem
and deep-seated bulb.

Flowers are large, nodding, and showy,
with 6 recurved, golden yellow tepals
(petals and sepals undifferentiated) and
colorful, protruding anthers and pistil.

Leaves (2) are large (to 8" long), shiny,
with sheathed bases.

Found in western Colorado in moist
situations, near snow banks, along
streams, and in meadows, forest openings, and aspen groves. Please protect
this lovely flower.

Life Zones: Montane to Alpine

Flowering Time: April to August

American Dwarf Mistletoe

(Pine Mistletoe, Dwarf Mistletoe)

Arceuthobium americanum
(Razoumofskya americana)

Mistletoe Family (Viscaceae)

Parasite on lodgepole pine, to 2¼"
high, in bunches, with yellowish,
fleshy stems that are segmented and
have whorled, angular branches.

Flowers are small and inconspicuous.
Male flowers are borne on stalklike
segments; female flowers are whorled
and protrude from nodes. The fruits
are berrylike, bluish or purplish green,
sticky, and fleshy, and they explode
when ripe.

Leaves are scalelike and opposite.

Grows only on lodgepole pines;
this parasite can kill the host tree.

Life Zones: Montane and Subalpine

Flowering Time: April to June

Dwarf Mistletoe

(Pine Mistletoe)

Arceuthobium vaginatum cryptopodum

Mistletoe Family (Viscaceae)

Harmful parasite on ponderosa pine, to 6" high, yellow overall but also greenish and brownish.

Flowers are inconspicuous, yellowish, nestling in axils; the plant shoots out sticky seeds 40' or more.

Leaves are reduced to scales.

Grows on twigs of ponderosa pine; this parasite can kill the tree.

Life Zones:
Foothills and Montane

Flowering Time: April to June

Alpine Wallflower

(Treakle Mustard, Prairie Rocket)

Erysimum capitatum
(E. nivale, E. radicatum)

Mustard Family (Brassicaceae)

Perennial, to 20" tall, fragrant, with erect, unbranched stem.

Flowers are in rounded, showy clusters, with 4 reflexed, deep orange to maroon or yellow petals. Seed pods are slender, to 3" long, and 4-angled.

Leaves are mostly basal, to 3" long, grayish green, with small teeth.

Common on rocky, gravelly slopes and hillsides, along ridges, and in forest openings.

Life Zones: Montane to Alpine

Flowering Time: May to August

Golden Draba

Draba aurea
(D. luteola, D. decumbens, D. aureiformis)

Mustard Family (Brassicaceae)

Perennial, to 6" tall, with erect, hairy, leafy stem.

Flowers are clustered, with 4 bright yellow petals and 4 hairy sepals. Seed pods are flat, to ½" long, and hairy.

Leaves are thick, oval to spoon-shaped, to 2" long, and hairy.

Common on slopes and in open woods, forest clearings, and rocky meadows.

Life Zones: Montane to Alpine

Flowering Time: June to August

Twisted-Pod Draba

Draba streptocarpa

Mustard Family (Brassicaceae)

Perennial, to 6" tall, with velvety, erect or twisted stems.

Flowers are clustered, with 4 golden yellow petals and 4 small, hairy sepals. Seed pods are twisted and velvety.

Leaves are silky; basal leaves are up to 1¼" long.

Common in open woods, forest clearings, and meadows, and on rocky, gravelly slopes.

Life Zones: Montane to Alpine

Flowering Time: June to August

Yellow Lady's Slipper

(Lady's Slipper, Moccasin Flower, Golden
 Lady's Slipper, Small Lady's Slipper)

*Cypripedium calceolus
parviflorum
(C. parviflorum, C. pubescens,
 C. veganum)*

Orchid Family (Orchidaceae)

Perennial, to 20" tall, with
downy, stout, erect but twisted stem.

Flowers are spectacular and fragrant,
with 3 ribbonlike sepals that are
twisted and tan and 2 petals similar
to the sepals. The third petal is
the "slipper" or "moccasin." It
is bright yellow, to 2" long, and
dotted inside with reddish to
purplish spots.

Leaves (to 5) are alternate and large
(to 6" by 3").

Grows in moist areas, such as bogs, marshes,
stream banks, and pond shores, but also in aspen
groves and forest clearings. Please don't molest
this beauty; it is getting rare in Colorado.

Life Zones: Foothills to Subalpine

Flowering Time: May to August

Alpine Avens

Acomastylis rossii turbinata
(Geum turbinatum,
Sieversia turbinata)

Rose Family (Rosaceae)

Perennial, to 10" tall, in dense mats, with thick rootstock and slender stems.

Flowers (several) are ¾" across, with 5 roundish, bright yellow petals and 5 pointed, green and purplish sepals.

Leaves are dark green, to 6" long, and pinnately divided into ½" long, toothed leaflets.

Found in vast patches, coloring slopes and hillsides golden yellow in summer and turning the tundra deep red in late summer.

Life Zones:
Subalpine and Alpine

Flowering Time:
June to August

221

Bur Avens

(Large-Leaved Avens)

Geum macrophyllum

Rose Family (Rosaceae)

Perennial, to 3' tall, with erect, hairy stem.

Flowers to ½" across, with 5 bright yellow petals and 5 pointed, drooping sepals. Fruit is burlike and bristly.

Leaves are divided into many leaflets of different sizes; the terminal leaflet is large and 3-parted.

Grows in moist areas of meadows, stream banks, and forests.

Life Zones: Foothills to Subalpine

Flowering Time: June to August

Beautiful Cinquefoil

(Beauty Potentilla)

Potentilla pulcherrima
(P. filipes)

Rose Family (Rosaceae)

Perennial, to 2' tall, with slender, erect stem.

Flowers to ¾" across, in clusters, with 5 yellow petals and 5 bristly sepals.

Leaves are long-stalked and divided into as many as 11 leaflets that are toothed and whitish and woolly beneath.

Prefers moist sites along ridges and hillsides, and in meadows.

Life Zones: Montane to Alpine

Flowering Time:
June to September

Blueleaf Cinquefoil

(Varileaf Cinquefoil, Glaucous
 Cinquefoil)

Potentilla diversifolia
(P. glaucophylla, P. intermittens)

Rose Family (Rosaceae)

Perennial, to 20" tall, tufted,
with stout rootstock and slender,
erect to spreading stems.

Flowers (to 5 per stem) are
½" across, with 5 bright yellow,
roundish, indented petals, 5 green
sepals, and 5 green bractlets.

Leaves are bluish green on
top, silky and grayish beneath,
and divided into 5 or 7 toothed
leaflets.

Grows in moist areas of valleys,
meadows, stream banks, and
pond shores.

Life Zones:
Subalpine and Alpine

Flowering Time:
June to August

Leafy Cinquefoil
(Wood Beauty)

Drymocallis fissa
(Potentilla fissa)

Rose Family (Rosaceae)

Perennial, to 12" tall, with leafy, sticky stems.

Flowers are large, 1" across, and clustered, with 5 bright yellow to creamy white petals, 5 green sepals, and 5 green bractlets.

Leaves are divided into as many as 13 sharp-toothed, sticky, and hairy leaflets.

Common in forest clearings, along roads, and on gravelly slopes.

Life Zones:
Foothills to Subalpine

Flowering Time:
May to August

Paired Cinquefoil

Potentilla subjuga

Rose Family (Rosaceae)

Perennial, to 12" high, with many stems in tufts.

Flowers to ½" across, with 5 bright yellow petals, hairy sepals, and up to 7 threadlike styles.

Leaves are palmately lobed into 5 leaflets and another pair below; all are toothed, dark green on top, and whitish and woolly beneath.

Grows on gravelly slopes, rocky ridges, and meadows.

Life Zones:
Subalpine and Alpine

Flowering Time:
July to September

Prairie Cinquefoil

Potentilla pensylvanica
(P. strigosa)

Rose Family (Rosaceae)

Perennial, in tufts, to 20" tall, with woody root and grayish, hairy stems.

Flowers are ½" across, have 5 pale yellow petals, and are in clusters.

Leaves are pinnately divided into as many as 15 leaflets that are about 2" long, deeply lobed and hairy to woolly.

Prefers dry environments in prairies, fields, and meadows, on slopes, and along bluffs.

Life Zones: Plains to Subalpine

Flowering Time: May to July

Redstem Cinquefoil

Potentilla rubricaulis
(P. tenerrima, P. minutifolia,
* P. saximontana, P. rubripes)*

Rose Family (Rosaceae)

Perennial, to 8" tall, tufted, with slender, reddish stems.

Flowers (several per plant) are on slender stalks, with 5 bright yellow, indented petals and 5 sepals, plus 5 bractlets that are pointed and woolly.

Leaves are mostly basal, stalked, and divided into 5 or 7 toothed leaflets that are deep green on top and woolly and white beneath.

Common on hillsides and tundra ridges and slopes, and along roads and trails.

Life Zones: Subalpine and Alpine

Flowering Time: July and August

Sticky Cinquefoil
(Tall Cinquefoil)

Drymocallis arguta
(Potentilla arguta)

Rose Family (Rosaceae)

Perennial, to 3' tall, with stout, sticky, hairy stems.

Flowers are in small clusters, with 5 yellow to creamy white petals.

Leaves are alternate and dissected into 3 to 9 lobes that are to 3½" long, hairy, and coarse-toothed.

Grows in meadows and forest clearings, and on grassy slopes.

Life Zones: Montane and Subalpine

Flowering Time: June to August

Woolly Cinquefoil

(Silvery Cinquefoil, Silvery Potentilla)

Potentilla hippiana

Rose Family (Rosaceae)

Perennial, to 20" high, in tufts, with slender, whitish, hairy, erect but leaning or curving stems.

Flowers are ½" across, in clusters, with 5 lemon yellow petals.

Leaves are divided into 13 or fewer toothed leaflets that are silvery and hairy on top and densely woolly beneath.

Common on dry ground on hillsides and gravelly slopes, in fields, and at forest borders.

Life Zones: Foothills to Subalpine

Flowering Time: June to August

Sibbaldia

(Creeping Sibbaldia, Clover-Leaved Rose)

Sibbaldia procumbens

Rose Family (Rosaceae)

Perennial, to 4" high, mat-forming, with creeping rootstock and slender stems.

Flowers are in tight clusters, with 5 narrow, toothed, yellow petals and 5 green, hairy sepals.

Leaves are dark green, basal, on long stalks, and divided into 3 lobes with broad, toothed tips.

Very common but often overlooked near snow banks, on rocky slopes, and in meadows and disturbed areas.

Life Zone: Alpine

Flowering Time: June and July

Silverweed

(Common Silverweed)

Argentina anserina

Rose Family (Rosaceae)

Perennial, to 5' long, creeping, with runners; stalks to 6" high.

Flowers to ¾" wide, with 5 roundish, bright yellow petals and more than 20 stamens.

Leaves are pinnately compound, to 10" long, with as many as 15 pairs of toothed leaflets that are silky white underneath.

Grows in moist ground along streams and rivers, on lake shores, and in meadows.

Life Zones: Plains to Subalpine

Flowering Time: May to July

Common Alumroot

(Small-Leaved Alumroot)

Heuchera parvifolia
(H. flavescens, H. utahensis)

Saxifrage Family (Saxifragaceae)

Perennial, to 2' tall, in clumps, with long, slender, sticky, reddish stems.

Flowers are tiny and clustered in long, spikelike panicles, with 5 pale yellow petals and 5 green to reddish, reflexed sepals.

Leaves, in basal rosette, are kidney-shaped but palmately segmented into as many as 9 bristly, hairy, toothed lobes.

Prefers dry and exposed sites, such as cliffs, gravelly hillsides, rocky slopes, outcrops, and boulder fields.

Life Zones: Plains to Subalpine

Flowering Time: May to August

Arctic Saxifrage

(Golden Saxifrage)

Hirculus prorepens
(Saxifraga hirculus, Leptacea hirculus)

Saxifrage Family (Saxifragaceae)

Perennial, to 8" tall, with erect or leaning, leafy stem.

Flowers are single, to ¾" across, with 5 golden yellow petals and 5 fleshy, green sepals with bristly margins.

Leaves are fleshy, to 1" long, spatulate, and smooth.

Grows in wet places, such as bogs, marshes, and melt basins, but also on exposed slopes.

Life Zones: Subalpine and Alpine

Flowering Time: July and August

Goldbloom Saxifrage

(Fairy Saxifrage, Golden Saxifrage)

Hirculus serpyllifolius chrysanthus
(Saxifraga serpyllifolia, S. chrysantha)

Saxifrage Family (Saxifragaceae)

Perennial, to 3" high, mat-forming, in clumps, with erect, curving stem.

Flowers are mostly single (rarely 2 or 3 per stem), ½" across, saucer-shaped; flowers have 5 clawed, bright yellow petals with red dots at the base and 5 fleshy, reflexed sepals.

Leaves to ½" long, fleshy, and smooth.

Grows in gravelly, rocky terrain on slopes and ridges.

Life Zones: Subalpine and Alpine

Flowering Time: July and August

Whiplash Saxifrage

Hirculus platysepalus crandallii
(Saxifraga flagellaris)

Saxifrage Family (Saxifragaceae)

Perennial, to 4" high, with white or red, stringy stolons and bristly, sticky, purplish stems.

Flowers to ½", to 3 per stem, with 5 bright yellow petals and 5 sticky, hairy, greenish and whitish sepals.

Leaves are fleshy and sticky, with toothed and bristly margins.

Common on tundra ridges and gravelly slopes, and in rock crevices.

Life Zone: Alpine

Flowering Time: July and August

Yellow Stonecrop

(Orpine, Stonecrop)

Amerosedum lanceolatum
(Sedum lanceolatum,
S. stenopetalum)

Stonecrop Family (Crassulaceae)

Perennial, to 8" tall, with slender rootstock and erect, fleshy stem.

Flowers are in clusters, with 5 pointed, bright yellow petals, 5 sharply pointed sepals, and 10 protruding stamens.

Leaves are alternate, to ¾" long, smooth, and fleshy.

Grows in open, sunny areas, such as prairies, tundra, rocky and gravelly slopes, trails, and roadsides.

Life Zones: Plains to Alpine

Flowering Time: June to August

Yellow Violet

(Johnny Jumpup, Yellow Prairie
Violet, Prairie Violet, Valley Yellow
Violet, Nuttall Violet, Wild Pansy)

Viola nuttallii

Violet Family (Violaceae)

Perennial, to 8" tall, in tufts,
with erect, leafy stems.

Flowers are ½" across and
nodding, with 5 bright yellow
petals that have brownish to
purplish veins.

Leaves have long stalks and
pointed tips.

Common in open fields and
clearings, on prairies and hillsides, and along forest borders.

Life Zones: Plains to Subalpine

Flowering Time: April to July

Colorado Currant

(Subalpine Black Currant)

Ribes coloradense

Gooseberry Family
(Grossulariaceae)

Low shrub, with spreading, crawling branches and brown bark.

Flowers are saucer-shaped, with spreading, sticky, hairy sepals and tubular corolla whose lobes are pink with purplish or greenish tinges. Berries are purplish black, sticky, to ⅜" across.

Leaves to 3" wide and cut into 5 toothed lobes that are hairy beneath.

Grows in woods, forest openings, canyons, and ravines.

Life Zones:
Montane and Subalpine

Flowering Time:
July and August

Wax Currant

(Squaw Currant)

Ribes cereum

Gooseberry Family
(Grossulariaceae)

Shrub, to 5' high, much-branched, sticky, and hairy.

Flowers are pink, tubular, about ¼" long, in small clusters. Berries are red, sticky, translucent.

Leaves are lobed, toothed, to 1⅛" across, aromatic.

Grows in dry gulches and on sunny slopes and canyon sides.

Life Zones:
Foothills and Montane

Flowering Time:
June to August

Wild Gooseberry

(Common Gooseberry, Mountain
  Gooseberry, White-Stemmed Gooseberry)

Ribes inerme
(R. vallicola, Grossularia inermis,
 G. purpusi)

Gooseberry Family (Grossulariaceae)

Shrub, to 3' high, with smooth, pale
twigs that bear some unequal spines.

Flowers are bell-shaped, with short,
pinkish and whitish petals. Berries
are reddish to purplish, to ⁵⁄₁₆" long,
and smooth.

Leaves are deeply cut into toothed
lobes that are smooth on top and
downy beneath.

Grows in moist, shady areas, in forest
openings, and along roads.

Life Zones: Foothills to Subalpine

Flowering Time: June to August

Dwarf Blueberry

(Dwarf Bilberry)

Vaccinium cespitosum

Heath Family (Ericaceae)

Shrub, to 12" high, with brown, velvety, round branches.

Flowers are urn-shaped, nodding, red, pinkish, or whitish, with no sepals. Berries are ¼" across, blue, juicy, and edible.

Leaves are oval, to 1½" long, thin, smooth, shiny, and toothed.

Grows as ground cover in forests, on stream banks, and along pond shores.

Life Zones: Subalpine and Alpine

Flowering Time: July and August

Mountain Laurel

(Alpine Laurel, Swamp Laurel, Bog Laurel, Pale Laurel, Bog Kalmia, Alpine Mountain Laurel)

Kalmia microphylla
(K. polifolia)

Heath Family (Ericaceae)

Shrub, to 18" tall, with much-branched, creeping stem.

Flowers are showy, to ¾" across, saucer-shaped, stalked, in loose clusters, with 5 bright pink to lavender petals.

Leaves are opposite, evergreen, leathery, dark green above, and white and hairy beneath.

Grows in cold, moist areas, such as meadows, bogs, swamps, lake shores, and stream banks.

Life Zones: Subalpine and Alpine

Flowering Time: July and August

Bush Honeysuckle

(Twinberry Honeysuckle, Swamp Honeysuckle,
Involucred Honeysuckle, Bracted Honeysuckle,
Twinberry, Black Twinberry, Bearberry,
Bearberry Honeysuckle)

Distegia involucrata
(Lonicera involucrata)

Honeysuckle Family (Caprifoliaceae)

Shrub, to 9' tall, with erect to reclining, gray, leafy stems.

Flowers are in pairs, with creamy yellow, tubular corolla and ½" long red bracts. Berries are round, ¼" across, black, and shiny; berries are subtended by persistent, red bracts.

Leaves are large (to 6" long), opposite, leathery, and hairy underneath, with pointed tips.

Common in wet places, such as stream banks, swamps, and bogs, and in forest clearings.

Life Zones: Foothills to Subalpine

Flowering Time: June to August

244

Twinflower

(American Twinflower)

Linnaea borealis
(L. americana)

Honeysuckle Family (Caprifoliaceae)

Dwarf shrub, mat-forming, with prostrate creeping stems whose flower-bearing branches are erect, slender, and to 6" high.

Flowers are paired, nodding, on slender, hairy stalks, narrowly bell-shaped, pink and white, and to ½" across.

Leaves are ovate to round, shiny and evergreen, stalked, to 1" long, and often wavy to toothed around tips.

Grows in moist, cool conifer forests; along streams, in bogs, near springs; on pondshores, and often in moss carpets. This forest elf is named after Carolus Linnaeus, the Swedish botanist who devised the binomial system for naming plants and animals.

Life Zones: Montane to Subalpine

Flowering Time: July to September

Prickly Rose

(Wild Rose)

Rosa sayi
(R. acicularis)

Rose Family (Rosaceae)

Shrub, to 5' tall, in patches, with horizontal rootstock and bristly, prickly stems and branches.

Flowers are large (to 2½" across), with 5 pink to reddish petals and 5 sticky, erect sepals. The fruit (hip) is pear-shaped, to ¾" long, red, with constricted neck.

Leaves are divided into as many as 9 leaflets that are 1" long, hairy beneath, with toothed margins. The stipules are large, with sticky hairs and bristly margins.

Grows in thickets and clearings, and on forest borders and rocky slopes.

Life Zones: Foothills to Subalpine

Flowering Time: June and July

Wild Rose

(Woods Rose, Native Rose)
Rosa woodsii

Rose Family (Rosaceae)

Shrub, to 6' tall, with thorny, prickly stems.

Flowers to 2½" across, with 5 deep pink petals, 5 sticky calyx lobes, and conspicuously protruding, yellow stamens and pistils. Fruit (hip) is red and hard; the fruit overwinters.

Leaves are compound (to 9 leaflets), toothed, with winged stalks.

Grows along roads and trails, on hillsides, and in draws and sunny, open valleys.

Life Zones:
Plains to Subalpine

Flowering Time:
June to August

Orange Agoseris

(Burnt Orange Agoseris, Burnt Orange
 Dandelion)

Agoseris aurantiaca
(A. gracilens, A. purpurea)

Aster Family (Asteraceae)

Perennial, to 2' tall, with milky sap,
stout taproot, and erect, curved stems.

Flower heads are 1" across, with no
disk flowers, deep orange to purplish
ray flowers, and tiered, overlapping,
slender bracts.

Leaves are basal, dark green, to
14" long, and somewhat lobed
or toothed.

Grows in forest openings, on grassy
slopes and hillsides, and along roads.

Life Zones: Foothills to Alpine

Flowering Time: June to August

Pink Pussytoes

(Rosy Pussytoes, Rosy Everlasting,
Pink Everlasting, Meadow Pussytoes,
Ladies' Tobacco)

Antennaria rosea
(A. imbricata)

Aster Family (Asteraceae)

Perennial, forms large mats via runners, with erect, white, woolly stems to 18" tall.

Flower heads have no ray flowers; male and female heads are on separate plants. The flower heads are crowded into roundish, woolly clusters with papery, whitish bracts whose tips are reddish.

Leaves are mostly basal, in rosette, to ¾" long, spatulate, and woolly.

Abundant in meadows and forest openings, along streams and roads, and on hillsides.

Life Zones: Foothills to Subalpine

Flowering Time: May to August

Red Anemone

(Red Windflower, Globe Anemone,
 Cliff Anemone, Cut-Leaved Anemone,
 Pacific Anemone)

Anemone multifida globosa
(A. globosa, A. tetonensis)

Buttercup Family (Ranunculaceae)

Perennial, in clumps from thick
rootstock, with slender, silky stems
to 18" tall.

Flowers to ¾" across, without petals
but with as many as 9 petal-like sepals
that are red to pink or magenta, even
greenish yellow. Seed heads are oval,
to ⅝" long.

Leaves are deeply and palmately
dissected into 5 main segments,
which are split into slender, linear
leaflets.

Common in rocky places, dry
meadows and forest openings, on
grassy slopes, and along roads.

Life Zones: Foothills to Alpine

Flowering Time: May to August

Spreading Dogbane

(Spreading Hemp, Indian Hemp,
  Rosy Dogbane)

Apocynum androsaemifolium

Dogbane Family (Apocynaceae)

Perennial, to 2' tall, with milky sap and smooth, erect stems.

Flowers are small (⅜"), bell-shaped, in small clusters; the 5 petals are white with red veins, and the 5 sepals are short and green.

Leaves are opposite, oval, to 3" long, and shiny on top.

Common along roads and trails, on rocky slopes and hillsides, and in open conifer woods. *Poisonous* sap.

Life Zones: Foothills to Subalpine

Flowering Time:
June to September

Alpine Fireweed

(Low Fireweed, Broadleaved Fireweed,
Broadleaved Willowherb, Dwarf Fireweed,
Red Willowherb, River Beauty)

Chamerion subdentatum
*(C. latifolium, Chamaenerion latifolium,
Epilobium latifolium)*

Evening Primrose Family (Onagraceae)

Perennial, to 20" tall, with several
leaning stems.

Flowers are large, showy, in short
racemes, with deep pink, 1" petals
and red, ½" sepals. Seed pods are
slender, to 1½" long.

Leaves are opposite, oval, thick,
to 2½" long, with grayish bloom
and minutely toothed margins.

Prefers moist ground along stream
banks and lake shores, and on talus
slopes and tundra.

Life Zones: Montane to Alpine

Flowering Time: June to September

Fireweed
(Willowweed, Willowherb, Blooming Sally)

Chamerion angustifolium
(Chamaenerion angustifolium,
Epilobium angustifolium)

Evening Primrose Family
(Onagraceae)

Perennial, to 6' high, in large patches, with horizontal rootstock and erect, shiny stems.

Flowers to 1" or more, with 4 roundish, pink to red or purplish petals and 4 linear sepals. Seed pods are slender, to 3" long, and 4-angled; the seeds are tufted, with silky, white hairs.

Leaves are lance-shaped, to 8" long, with wavy or weakly toothed margins.

Abundant along roads, in burned areas and forest openings, on cleared land, and at the edges of woods.

Life Zones: Foothills to Subalpine

Flowering Time: June to September

Little Red Elephant

(Elephant Heads, Elephant Flower)

Pedicularis groenlandica
(Elephantella groenlandica)

Figwort Family (Scrophulariaceae)

Perennial, to 2' tall, in large colonies, with erect, leafy, purplish stems.

Flowers are pink, reddish, or purplish, in dense, long spikes. Flowers are 2-lipped; the upper lip is long and curving (the "elephant trunk"), and the lower lip has 3 lobes.

Leaves are narrow, to 6" long, fleshy, purplish, and pinnately divided into narrow, toothed lobes.

Found in shallow water, wet meadows, bogs, and swamps, and near streams, ponds, and springs.

Life Zones: Montane to Alpine

Flowering Time: June to August

Rosy Paintbrush

(Subalpine Paintbrush, Splitleaf Paintbrush)

Castilleja rhexifolia
(C. humilis, C. lauta, C. obtusiloba)

Figwort Family (Scrophulariaceae)

Perennial, to 20" tall, in clumps, with erect, unbranched stems.

Flowers are small, yellowish green, in tight cluster hidden by large, 3-lobed bracts that are conspicuous, magenta, pink, purple, or red.

Leaves to 2½" long and strongly 3-nerved; upper leaves may be lobed.

Common in forest openings and on tundra slopes, hillsides, and meadows.

Life Zones: Subalpine and Alpine

Flowering Time: June to August

Scarlet Paintbrush

(Indian Paintbrush, Great Red Paintbrush,
 Giant Red Paintbrush)

Castilleja miniata

Figwort Family (Scrophulariaceae)

Perennial, to 3' tall, with sticky, hairy stem.

Flowers are in a dense cluster, with a tubular, 2-lipped, green corolla and bright red, 3-lobed bracts.

Leaves are alternate, broadly lance-shaped, to 4" long; the upper leaves are 3-lobed.

Common in moist meadows, open woods, aspen groves, and forest openings, and along streams.

Life Zones: Foothills to Subalpine

Flowering Time: May to September

Wyoming Paintbrush

(Narrowleaf Paintbrush)

Castilleja linariaefolia

Figwort Family
(Scrophulariaceae)

Perennial, to 3' tall, with branched stems.

Flowers are in a cluster, with a tubular, yellowish and reddish corolla and bright red or orange bracts that are deeply cleft.

Leaves are linear, 3-lobed.

Grows in sunny areas, such as forest openings, meadows, sagebrush slopes, and aspen groves. This is the state flower of Wyoming.

Life Zones:
Foothills and Montane

Flowering Time: June to August

Strawberry Blite

(Indian Paint, Squaw Paint)

Chenopodium capitatum
(Blitum capitatum)

Goosefoot Family (Chenopodiaceae)

Annual, to 16" tall, with erect, smooth stem.

Flowers are tiny, in tight clusters, with no petals; cleft, green sepals turn bright red later in the year.

Leaves are alternate, triangular, smooth, and coarsely toothed; they turn bright red late in the season.

Found along roads and trails, in burned areas and forest clearings, on gravelly hillsides, and around abandoned buildings.

Life Zones: Montane and Subalpine

Flowering Time: June to August

Red Columbine

(Crimson Columbine, Rocky Mountain Red Columbine)

Aquilegia elegantula

Hellebore Family (Helleboraceae)

Perennial, 16" tall, with slender, erect stems.

Flowers to 2" long, drooping, with 5 red, spoon-shaped petals that stretch into straight, slender, red or yellow spurs. The 5 sepals are elliptical and red and yellow.

Leaves are mostly basal, delicate, bluish green, and deeply cleft into 3 segments, which in turn are divided into rounded leaflets.

Prefers moist soils on the Western Slope, where it graces woody hillsides, forest edges, and openings. This beauty is one of Colorado's gems and must be preserved for later generations.

Life Zones: Montane and Subalpine

Flowering Time: June to August

Alpine Sorrel

(Mountain Sorrel,
 Alpine Mountain Sorrel)

Oxyria digyna

Knotweed Family (Polygonaceae)

Perennial, to 10" tall, with thick taproot and fleshy, ribbed stems.

Flowers are tiny (¹⁄₁₆"), in tight raceme, with red petals and green sepals.

Leaves are fleshy, long-stalked, sour tasting, with kidney-shaped blades.

Found in wet, shady areas, such as tundra rills and depressions, forest edges, and rock crevices.

Life Zones: Subalpine and Alpine

Flowering Time: July to September

Subalpine Buckwheat

(Umbrella Plant, Wild Buckwheat, Indian
 Tobacco, Creamy Sulphur Flower)

Eriogonum subalpinum

Knotweed Family (Polygonaceae)

Perennial, to 8" tall, in patches,
with stout, erect, hairy stems.

Flowers are in small clusters that
form umbels, which are subtended by
leaflike bracts. Flowers have no petals;
the 6 sepals are reddish to whitish.

Leaves are basal, in rosette, thick,
spatulate, and woolly underneath.

Grows abundantly in meadows, along
ridges, and on hillsides and rocky,
gravelly slopes.

Life Zones: Montane and Subalpine

Flowering Time: June to September

Wood Lily

(Rocky Mountain Lily, Red Lily)
Lilium philadelphicum

Lily Family (Liliaceae)

Perennial, to 2' tall, with bulb and erect, leafy stem.

Flowers are striking, to 2½" across, orange to bright red, with 6 tepals (petals indistinguishable from sepals), and purple anthers.

Leaves are broadly linear, to 4" long.

Grows in moist meadows, aspen groves, and forest openings. This beauty is endangered and rare.

Life Zones:
Foothills and Montane

Flowering Time:
June and July

Charming Wallflower
(Alpine Wallflower)

Erysimum amoenum
(E. wheeleri)

Mustard Family (Brassicaceae)

Perennial, to 6" tall, in tight clumps, with woody root and erect, curved, purplish stem.

Flowers are fragrant, in open clusters, with 4 clawed, magenta, reddish, or purplish petals. Seed pods are slender and hairy.

Leaves are mostly basal, fleshy, and narrow, with wavy or toothed margins.

Grows in gravelly and rocky tundra, and on slopes and ridges.

Life Zones: Subalpine and Alpine

Flowering Time: June and July

Geyer Onion

(Wild Onion)

Allium geyeri
(A. dictyotum, A. funiculosum,
A. pikeanum)

Onion Family (Alliaceae)

Perennial, to 20" tall (dwarfed above timberline), with onion smell. The single, stout stem arises from a small, underground bulb.

Flowers are small (³⁄₁₆"), in a small umbel, with pink to lavender or whitish petals and papery bracts.

Leaves (usually 3), are slender, folded, and as long as the stem.

Grows along rills and in moist meadows, swales, and forest openings.

Life Zones: Foothills to Alpine

Flowering Time: June to August

Nodding Onion

(Wild Onion)

Allium cernuum
(A. recurvatum,
A. neomexicanum)

Onion Family (Alliaceae)

Perennial, to 20" tall, with purplish bulb and slender, erect stem.

Flowers are drooping, on long stalks, forming an umbel, with 6 roundish petals that are pink, lavender, and whitish.

Leaves are basal, to 10" long, smooth, and grasslike.

Grows in moist places in woods, on grassy slopes, and along ledges and ridges.

Life Zones: Foothills to Subalpine

Flowering Time: May to October

Wild Chives

(Siberian Chives)

Allium schoenoprasum
(A. sibiricum)

Onion Family (Alliaceae)

Perennial, to 18" tall (dwarfed above timberline), with onion smell, 2 white bulbs (often), and slender, erect stem.

Flowers to ½" long, pink or lavender, in roundish umbel subtended by cleft, papery bracts.

Leaves (2) are slender, round, smooth, and shorter than the stem.

Grows in mountain parks, forest clearings, valleys, and meadows, and along tundra rills.

Life Zones: Montane to Alpine

Flowering Time: June to August

Fairy Slipper

(Calypso Orchid, Calypso, Venus' Slipper)

Calypso bulbosa
(C. borealis, Cytheria bulbosa)

Orchid Family (Orchidaceae)

Perennial, in patches, to 8" tall, with erect, smooth, reddish, sheathed stems.

Flowers to 1½" across, drooping, with 3 slender, pink sepals; 2 petals are similar to the sepals, but the third petal is expanded into the "slipper," which is 1" long, pink and white, with purple splotches.

Leaf is single, basal, to 2½" long, and bluish green.

Grows in bogs and mossy mounds in forests, and near springs and seeps. This spectacular orchid is endangered and must be protected.

Life Zones: Foothills to Subalpine

Flowering Time: April to July

267

Spotted Coralroot

(Mottled Coral-Root, Summer Coral-Root)

Corallorhiza maculata

Orchid Family (Orchidaceae)

Perennial, with fleshy, 20" stems. This plant lacks chlorophyll and is leafless; it grows on a fungus, which it uses for a root system.

Flowers to ¾" long, in terminal raceme, with 3 dark red, petal-like sepals and 2 similar petals, plus a third large, white, red-dotted petal.

Found in aspen groves and among conifers.

Life Zones: Foothills to Subalpine

Flowering Time: May to August

Dwarf Clover
(Deer Clover)
Trifolium nanum
Pea Family (Fabaceae)

Perennial, to 2" high, mat-forming, with smooth, leafless stems.

Flowers are large (¾" long), in loose clusters, erect, reddish, purplish, and whitish.

Leaves are basal, stalked, fleshy, smooth, slightly toothed, and sharply pointed.

Grows in meadows and on gravelly slopes and rocky ridges.

Life Zones:
Subalpine and Alpine

Flowering Time: June and July

Parry Clover

(Rose Clover)

Trifolium parryi
(T. montanense, T. salictorum)

Pea Family (Fabaceae)

Perennial, in clumps, to 6"
high, with arching, leafless,
smooth stems.

Flowers are ½" long, pink,
reddish, or purplish, in
roundish clusters subtended
by whitish bracts.

Leaves are basal, long-stalked,
smooth, and split into 3 sharp-
toothed leaflets.

Grows along streams and
forest borders, and in woods
openings and tundra swales.

Life Zones:
Subalpine and Alpine

Flowering Time:
July to September

Limber Vetch

(Wiry Milkvetch)

Astragalus flexuosus
(Homalobus flexuosus,
* Pisophaca flexuosa, P. elongata)*

Pea Family (Fabaceae)

Perennial, to 20" long, with spreading, wiry, tough, hairy stem.

Flowers are small (less than ½"), in one-sided racemes, pink or pale lavender, with black-haired calyx lobes. Seed pods are smooth and almost 1" long.

Leaves are pinnately divided into ½" long leaflets that are densely hairy beneath.

Common in dry areas, such as fields, slopes, hillsides, gulch banks, and the edges of thickets.

Life Zones: Foothills and Montane

Flowering Time: June and July

Fairy Trumpet

(Skyrocket, Scarlet Gilia,
 Skyrocket Gilia, Skunk Flower)

Ipomopsis aggregata
(Gilia aggregata)

Phlox Family (Polemoniaceae)

Biennial, to 5' tall, with slender, downy stem.

Flowers are in long, one-sided panicle, with bright red, trumpet-shaped corolla that is up to 2" long.

Leaves are alternate, to 2½" long, sticky, and pinnately dissected.

Grows in dry areas, such as sunny, open woods, rocky slopes, and fields. *Caution:* Plant is poisonous.

Life Zones:
Foothills and Montane

Flowering Time:
June to September

Pinedrops

(Giant Bird's Nest)

Pterospora andromedea

Pinesap Family (Monotropaceae)

Annual, without chlorophyll, to 3' tall, in clumps, with single, stout, sticky, reddish to purplish stem.

Flowers are bell-shaped and drooping, with red stalks and red and white corolla lobes.

Leaves are tannish brown, slender, to 1" long, hairy, and translucent.

Grows on organic debris in conifer forests.

Life Zones: Foothills and Montane

Flowering Time: June to August

Moss Campion

(Moss Pink, Cushion Pink,
 Dwarf Catchfly)

Silene acaulis subacaulescens

Pink Family (Caryophyllaceae)

Perennial, to 2" tall, in large, dense
mats, with erect to leaning stems.

Flowers are single, tubular, and
erect, with reflexed, pink to white
petals and reddish green, ⅜" long
calyx.

Leaves are basal, grasslike, bright
green, to 1½" long, with bristly
margins.

Grows on exposed ridges, slopes,
and hillsides, and in rock crevices.

Life Zone: Alpine
Flowering Time: June to August

274

Fairy Primrose

(Alpine Primrose)

Primula angustifolia

Primrose Family (Primulaceae)

Perennial, to 5" tall, in clumps, with erect, twisted stem.

Flowers are showy, ¾" across, fragrant, with 5 flaring, notched, reddish to purplish petals with yellow throats, and purplish green, hairy sepals.

Leaves are stalked, slender, fleshy, grayish green, and hairy.

Found in boulder fields, rock crevices, and meadows, near snow banks, and along rivulets.

Life Zones:
Subalpine and Alpine

Flowering Time:
June to August

Parry Primrose

(Alpine Primrose, Brook Primrose)

Primula parryi

Primrose Family (Primulaceae)

Perennial, to 16" tall, with stout, smooth, leafless, erect, and curving stem.

Flowers are showy, in elongate cluster, with tubular, 5-lobed corolla, whose reflexed lobes are 1" across, vivid magenta or purplish red, with yellow throats.

Leaves are basal, to 12" long, thick, fleshy, and smooth.

Grows along waterfalls and streams, near snow banks, around seeps, in swales and rock crevices, and among boulders.

Life Zones: Subalpine and Alpine

Flowering Time: June to August

Shooting Star

(American Cowslip, American
  Cyclamen)

Dodecatheon pulchellum
(D. pauciflorum)

Primrose Family (Primulaceae)

Perennial, to 16" tall, with erect,
fleshy stem.

Flowers to 1½" long, drooping,
with 4 or 5 bent-back petals that
are pink to purple and set off by
a yellow to purplish "beak" of
fused stamens.

Leaves are basal, to 12" long,
spatulate, and bright green.

Grows in cool, shady, wet places,
such as damp meadows, stream
banks, and forest glades.

Life Zones: Foothills to Subalpine

Flowering Time: April to July

Pygmy Bitterroot

(Bitterroot, Lewisia, Dwarf Lewisia,
Little Lewisia, Least Lewisia, Tiny
Lewisia, Pygmy Breadroot)

Oreobroma pygmaea
(Lewisia pygmaea)

Purslane Family (Portulacaceae)

Perennial, 2" high, with large
taproot.

Flowers to ¾" across,
with reddish pink, magenta,
or white petals and 2 fleshy,
toothed sepals.

Leaves are slender, to 2½"
long, basal, fleshy, and
spreading.

Common near wet spots,
such as snow banks, seeps,
damp forests, rills, and
streams.

Life Zones: Subalpine and Alpine

Flowering Time: June to August

Red Alumroot

(Jack-o'-the-Rocks)

Heuchera rubescens

Saxifrage Family (Saxifragaccac)

Perennial, in clumps, to 18" tall, with slender, erect, reddish, hairy stem.

Flowers are bell-shaped, in small, stalked clusters, with 5 tiny, pink and white petals and 5 reddish, hairy sepals.

Leaves are in basal rosette, with long, slender stalks and 5-lobed blades with toothed margins.

Grows in western Colorado among outcrops, cliffs, boulders, and granitic gravel.

Life Zones:
Montane and Subalpine

Flowering Time: May to July

King's Crown

(Roseroot, Western Roseroot)

Rhodiola integrifolia
(R. polygama, Sedum integrifolia,
S. rosea)

Stonecrop Family (Crassulaceae)

Perennial, to 12" tall, with fleshy,
red rootstock and stout, erect, fleshy,
leafy stem.

Flowers are in a terminal cluster, small
(⅛"), with 4 purple or reddish petals
and a 4-lobed, purple or reddish calyx.

Leaves are alternate, to 1" long, fleshy,
smooth, bluish green (red in fall), with
teeth around the tip.

Grows on lake shores and stream banks,
and in swales and rills on tundra.

Life Zones: Subalpine and Alpine

Flowering Time: June to August

280

Rose Crown

(Queen's Crown, Red Orpine)

Clementsia rhodantha
(Sedum rhodanthum)

Stonecrop Family (Crassulaceae)

Perennial, to 12" tall, in colonies, with stout rootstock and fleshy, stout, unbranched stem.

Flowers are in elongate, terminal cluster, with pink and white, pointed petals.

Leaves are slender, to 1" long, horizontal, somewhat fleshy, and bright red in fall.

Grows in bogs and seeps, and along streams and pond shores.

Life Zones: Subalpine and Alpine

Flowering Time: June to August

Bog Wintergreen

(Swamp Wintergreen, Pink Wintergreen, Pink
Pyrola, Swamp Pyrola, Pink Bog Pyrola, Alpine
Pyrola, Roundleaved Pyrola, Pinkflowered
Pyrola, Pink Swamp Pyrola, Shinleaf)

Pyrola rotundifolia asarifolia
(P. asarifolia, P. rotundifolia,
P. asarifolia purpurea, P. uliginosa)

Wintergreen Family (Pyrolaceae)

Perennial, to 16" tall, with slender,
flexible, smooth stem.

Flowers are nodding, stalked, in racemes,
with 5 roundish, pink, red, and white petals.

Leaves are basal, to 3½" long, with long
stalks; blades are thick, leathery, bright green
on top and brownish beneath, with small,
knoblike teeth on the margins.

Grows in wet areas, such as stream banks,
springs, bogs, forest glades, and willow thickets.

Life Zones: Montane and Subalpine

Flowering Time: June to August

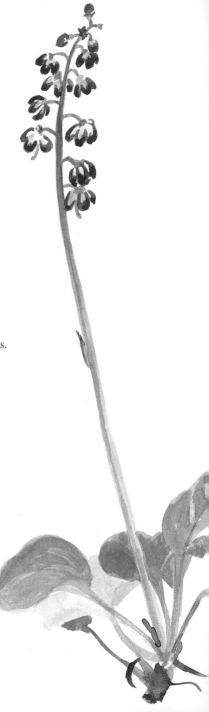

Alpine Forget-Me-Not
(Dwarf Forget-Me-Not, Moss Forget-Me-Not)

Eritrichum aretioides
(E. argenteum, E. elongatum, E. nanum)

Borage Family (Boraginaceae)

Perennial, mat-forming, fragrant, to 2" high, with slender, hairy stem.

Flowers are ¼" across, in terminal clusters, with a 5-lobed, tubular corolla that is blue or white with a yellow throat.

Leaves are basal, thick, fleshy, silvery, and hairy.

Found in open areas on ridge crests, rocky slopes, and disturbed tundra.

Life Zones: Subalpine and Alpine

Flowering Time: June to August

False Forget-Me-Not

(Wild Forget-Me-Not, Stickseed
Forget-Me-Not, Many-Flowered
Stickseed)

Hackelia floribunda

Borage Family (Boraginaceae)

Biennial, to 4' high, with stout,
hairy, fleshy stems.

Flowers are cup-shaped, ¼"
across, in drooping clusters, with
5 dull blue, spreading petals and
5 fleshy, hairy, dark green sepals.

Leaves to 6" long, narrowly lance-
shaped, fleshy, and grayish and
hairy beneath.

Grows in meadows, forest clearings, and aspen groves, among
shrubs, and on hillsides.

Life Zones: Foothills to Subalpine

Flowering Time: June to August

Tall Chiming Bells

(Tall Mertensia, Mountain
Bluebell, Languid Lady, Lungwort)

Mertensia ciliata
(M. picta, M. punctata,
M. pallida, M. polyphylla)

Borage Family
(Boraginaceae)

Perennial, to 4' tall,
in large clumps, with
erect, leafy, curved stems.

Flowers are bell-shaped, in
nodding clusters, with light
blue to pinkish corollas.

Leaves are alternate, soft, smooth,
to 6" long; upper leaves are sessile,
and lower leaves are stalked.

Grows on stream banks and
pond shores, and near springs
and seeps.

Life Zones: Montane to Alpine

Flowering Time: June to August

Alpine Speedwell

(American Alpine Speedwell,
 Alpine Veronica)

Veronica nutans
(V. wormskjoldia)

Figwort Family (Scrophulariaceae)

Perennial, to 12" tall, with erect,
curved, hairy stem.

Flowers are dainty, in a tight,
terminal cluster, with purplish
blue, rounded petals.

Leaves are opposite, oval, and
toothed.

Grows in wet areas, such as
swales, bogs, stream banks, seeps,
and rivulets.

Life Zones: Subalpine and Alpine

Flowering Time: July and August

Clustered Penstemon

(Little Penstemon, Small-Flowered Penstemon,
Littleflower Penstemon, Tinybloom Penstemon,
Blue Beardtongue)

Penstemon confertus procerus
(P. procerus, P. micranthes, Lepteiris parviflora)

Figwort Family (Scrophulariaceae)

Perennial, in clumps, to 16" tall, with woody
rootstock and slender, smooth, erect stem.

Flowers are small (⅜"), in compact, tiered
clusters. The upper lip is 2-lobed and the
lower 3-lobed, with colors ranging from light
blue to dark blue and purple.

Stem leaves are opposite, clasping, and
narrow; basal leaves are in rosette, lance-
shaped to oval, stalked, and hairy beneath.

Grows on grassy slopes and in meadows
and forest openings.

Life Zones: Montane to Alpine

Flowering Time: June to August

Low Penstemon

(Blue Mist Penstemon, Greenleaf Penstemon)

Penstemon virens

Figwort Family (Scrophulariaceae)

Perennial, to 10" high, in dense clumps, with erect, slender, hairy stems.

Flowers to ¾" long, tubular, and 2-lipped; the upper lip is pinkish, and the lower lip is bright blue and very hairy.

Leaves are light green and shiny; the basal leaves are stalked, to 3" long, and the upper leaves are clasping and hug the stem.

Common in rocky, gravelly areas, such as road banks and hillsides.

Life Zones: Foothills to Subalpine

Flowering Time: June to August

Rydberg Penstemon

Penstemon rydbergii
(P. erosus, P. lacerellus, P. latiusculus)

Figwort Family
(Scrophulariaceae)

Perennial, to 16" tall, in tufts, with erect stems that are bent at the base.

Flowers are small (to ½" long), dark blue, purple, or violet, in whorls that form clusters.

Stem leaves are opposite and clasping; basal leaves are stalked, spatulate, to 4" long, in a tight rosette.

Common in wet meadows, open woods, and thickets, and on grassy slopes.

Life Zones: Foothills to Subalpine

Flowering Time: June and July

Tall Penstemon

(Tall Beardtongue, One-Sided
Penstemon, Tall One-Sided
Penstemon)

Penstemon unilateralis
(P. virgata)

Figwort Family (Scrophulariaceae)

Perennial, to 30" tall, with stout,
unbranched, smooth stems.

Flowers are in one-sided racemes,
with bright blue to purplish,
tubular corolla that is 2-lipped.

Leaves to 4" long, broadly lance-
shaped, and smooth.

Conspicuous and abundant
along roads, in overgrazed pastures
and disturbed areas, and on sandy
hillsides.

Life Zones: Foothills and Montane

Flowering Time: June and July

Moss Gentian

(Siberian Gentian)

Chondrophylla prostrata
(Gentiana prostrata, G. chondrophylla)

Gentian Family (Gentianaceae)

Annual, to 3" tall, with slender, erect or prostrate, leafy stem.

Flowers are single, tubular, ¾" long; flowers usually have 4 pointed, blue to purplish corolla lobes that are joined by pointed pleats.

Leaves hug the stem and are smooth, less than ½" long.

Grows on grassy slopes and ridges, in meadows, and around bogs and ponds.

Life Zone: Alpine

Flowering Time: June to August

Mountain Gentian

(Blue Gentian, Pleated Gentian, Parry
Gentian, Bottle Gentian, Puff Gentian)

Pneumonanthe parryi
*(P. calycosa, Gentiana parryi, G. calycosa,
G. bracteosa, Dasystephana parryi)*

Gentian Family (Gentianaceae)

Perennial, to 15" tall, in clumps, with
erect, leafy stems.

Flowers are barrel-shaped, to 2" long,
with up to 3 flowers per stem. Flowers
have 5 narrow sepals and 5 petals fused
into the "barrel" or "bottle," which
splits into 5 pointed, reflexed lobes
and 5 smaller lobes or "pleats." Color
varies from azure blue to purple.

Leaves are opposite, to 1½" long,
broadly oval, bluish green, and smooth.

Prefers moist meadows, stream banks,
bogs, willow thickets, and forest borders.

Life Zones: Montane and Subalpine

Flowering Time: July to September

Colorado Columbine

(Blue Columbine, Colorado Blue
 Columbine, Rocky Mountain
 Columbine)

Aquilegia coerulea

Hellebore Family (Helleboraceae)

Perennial, to 3' tall, with erect,
slender, branched stem.

Flowers are spectacular, to 3"
across, with 5 spreading, blue
to lavender sepals and 5 scoop-
shaped, white petals that trail
slender blue spurs.

Leaves are mostly basal, with
long, slender stalks and blades,
deeply dissected into 1" long,
rounded lobes that are bluish
green underneath.

Prefers moist soil of ravines,
rocky slopes, willow thickets,
aspen groves, and forest clearings. This beauty deserves its
honor as Colorado's state flower.

Life Zones: Foothills to Alpine

Flowering Time: June to August

Blue Bonnet

(Baker Lupine)

Lupinus bakeri bakeri
(L. harbiger, L. dichrous)

Pea Family (Fabaceae)

Perennial, to 2' tall, in dense clumps, with tough, reddish stem.

Flowers are small (⅜"), with bluish purple lips and purple spur.

Leaves are palmately compound and divided into bluish green, soft, 2" long leaflets.

Grows on the Western Slope in meadows, sagebrush slopes, and open woods.

Life Zones: Foothills and Montane

Flowering Time: June and July

Lodgepole Lupine

Lupinus argenteus parviflorus
(L. parviflorus, L. floribundus)

Pea Family (Fabaceae)

Perennial, to 32" tall, with erect, leafy, silvery, hairy stems.

Flowers are pealike, many, less than 1½" long, and in racemes to 10" long, with blue or purple (sometimes also white or tan) corollas that have short keel tips. The bracts are hairy. The seed pods are 1" long and bear 4 or fewer seeds.

Leaves are palmately divided into folded leaflets (as many as 11, to 2½" long), bright green on top, and grayish and hairy beneath.

Common in meadows, aspen groves, and open woods, and on hillsides and slopes.

Life Zones: Foothills to Subalpine

Flowering Time: June to August

Silvery Lupine

Lupinus argenteus argenteus

Pea Family (Fabaceae)

Perennial, to 20" high, with woody rootstock and leafy, silvery, hairy, branched stems.

Flowers are pealike, arranged in narrow, twisted racemes to 7" long, with blue or purple (sometimes also white) corollas and silvery, hairy bracts. Corolla keels have slender, pointed tips. Seed pods are flat, to 1⅜" long, with 6 seeds.

Leaves are palmately divided into narrow leaflets (as many as 9) that are silvery and hairy beneath, less than 3" long.

Common in open woods, along roads, and on hillsides and slopes.

Life Zones: Foothills to Subalpine

Flowering Time: May to August

Jacob's Ladder

(Delicate Jacob's Ladder, Subalpine
 Jacob's Ladder, Showy Jacob's Ladder,
 Skunk Leaf)

*Polemonium pulcherrimum
delicatum*
(P. delicatum, P. scopulinum)

Phlox Family (Polemoniaceae)

Perennial, to 10" tall, with clusters
of weak, slender, woolly stems.

Flowers are smelly, in small clusters,
with 5 pale blue or violet (sometimes white or pinkish) petals and
5 green, pointed, hairy sepals.

Leaves are alternate and pinnately
dissected like a ladder into ½" long,
pale green leaflets.

Prefers shade; grows under conifers,
in thickets and moist meadows,
along streams, and among moss
hummocks and boulders.

Lie Zones: Subalpine and Alpine

Flowering Time: June to August

Sky Pilot

(Sticky Polemonium, Skunkweed)

Polemonium viscosum
(P. confertum, P. grayanum, P. mellitum)

Phlox Family (Polemoniaceae)

Perennial, to 10" high, in clumps, with erect, twisted, hairy, sticky stems.

Flowers are fragrant, funnel-shaped, in tight, terminal clusters, with 5 blue or lavender (sometimes white), roundish corolla lobes and a densely hairy calyx.

Leaves are mostly basal, to 6" long, narrow, and pinnately divided into many small, hairy, sticky, smelly leaflets.

Common on tundra slopes and crests, in boulder fields and disturbed meadows, and along trails.

Life Zone: Alpine

Flowering Time: June to August

Colorado Tansy Aster

Machaeranthera coloradoensis
(Aster coloradensis,
Xylorrhiza coloradensis)

Aster Family (Asteraceae)

Perennial, to 5" high, with woody taproot and erect to prostrate, hairy stem.

Flower heads are large (1½" across), with purple to lavender ray flowers, a yellow disk, and 3-tiered, pointed bracts.

Leaves are spatulate, densely hairy, and toothed.

Grows in gravelly and rocky areas, such as tundra slopes, open woods, boulder fields, and hillsides.

Life Zones: Montane to Alpine

Flowering Time: June to August

Common Aster

(Pacific Aster)

Aster adscendens
(A. ascendens, A. chilensis, A. nuttallii,
A. violaceus, A. nelsonii, A. underwoodii,
A. grisens)

Aster Family (Asteraceae)

Perennial, in clumps, to 30" high, with wiry, sticky, reddish stems.

Flower heads are 1" across, with pale lavender ray flowers, yellow disks, and 3 to 4 rows of bristly, green and white bracts.

Leaves are narrowly lance-shaped, to 5" long; lower leaves are stalked and spatulate.

Abundant in western and southern Colorado, in dry places such as gravelly slopes and flats, on hillsides, along roads, and in moist sites like marshes and pond shores.

Life Zones: Foothills to Subalpine

Flowering Time: July to September

Field Aster

(Prairie Aster)

Virgulus campestris
(Aster campestris)

Aster Family (Asteraceae)

Perennial, to 16" tall, with creeping rootstock and erect, slender, sticky stems.

Flower heads are many, bunched, with blue to purple ray flowers, small, yellow disks, and sticky bracts in 3 rows.

Leaves are narrow, to 1¼" long, and sticky.

Common on grassy slopes and in fields, open thickets, and woods.

Life Zones:
Montane and Subalpine

Flowering Time:
July to September

Leafy Aster

(Leafy-Bracted Aster)

Aster foliaceus
(A. phyllodes, A. tweedyi)

Aster Family (Asteraceae)

Perennial, to 3' tall, in clumps, with erect, reddish, leafy, and hairy stems.

Flower heads are large (to 2" across), with pinkish and lavender ray flowers, bright yellow disks, and hairy, leaflike bracts.

Leaves are broadly lance-shaped, to 8" long; the upper leaves are clasping, and the basal leaves are stalked.

Common along roads and pond shores, and in meadows, thickets, and forest openings.

Life Zones: Foothills to Subalpine

Flowering Time: July to September

Smooth Aster

(Sky-Blue Aster)

Aster laevis geyeri

Aster Family (Asteraceae)

Perennial, to 3' tall, with stout, erect, smooth stems.

Flower heads are 1" across, with many blue to lavender ray flowers, yellow to orange disks, and several tiers of whitish, green-tipped bracts. Flower heads are in clusters.

Leaves are broadly lance-shaped, to 8" long, thick, smooth, and bluish green.

Grows in meadows, open woods, and on slopes.

Life Zones: Plains to Montane

Flowering Time:
August to October

303

Sunloving Aster

(Leafy Aster, Leafy-Bracted Aster)

Aster foliaceus apricus
(A. apricus)

Aster Family (Asteraceae)

Perennial, to 10" tall, with rootstock, in clumps, with erect, leaning, purplish stem.

Flower heads are large (to 2" across), often nodding, with many indented, purple to pinkish ray flowers and large yellow disk; bracts are 3-tiered, green and purplish.

Leaves are large (to 4" long), smooth, and stalked; the upper leaves are reduced and clasping.

Grows in open areas, such as meadows, forest openings, slopes, and ridges.

Life Zones: Subalpine and Alpine

Flowering Time:
June to September

Tall Tansy Aster

(Bigelow Aster, Tansy Aster,
 Sticky Aster)

Machaeranthera bigelovii
(Aster bigelovii, A. aspera)

Aster Family (Asteraceae)

Biennial, to 6' tall, with erect, much-branched stem.

Flower heads are showy, 1½" across, with purple ray flowers, yellow to orange disks, and sticky bracts with recurved tips.

Leaves are narrowly lance-shaped, to 4" long, thick, sharply toothed, and smelly.

Common in disturbed ground, such as roadsides, trailheads, fields, and hillsides.

Life Zones:
Foothills and Montane

Flowering Time:
August to October

Tansy Aster

(Tall Tansy Aster, Patterson Tansy
Aster, Sticky Aster, Sticky Tansy Aster)

Machaeranthera pattersonii
(Aster pattersonii, A. aspera)

Aster Family (Asteraceae)

Perennial, to 3' tall, with taproot
and rough, woody, much-branched
stem.

Flower heads to 1½" across, with
purple to lavender or reddish ray
flowers, small, orange to yellow
disks, and recurved, green and
white, sticky bracts.

Leaves to 3½" long, thick, and
linear, with pointed tips and several
sharp teeth.

Common along roads and trails,
in disturbed ground around picnic
areas, and in fields and open woods.

Life Zones: Foothills to Subalpine

Flowering Time:
August to November

One-Headed Daisy

(One-Flowered Daisy)

Erigeron simplex
(E. leucotrichus)

Aster Family (Asteraceae)

Perennial, to 10" tall, with simple, erect, and hairy stem.

Flower head single, to 1" wide, with many bluish violet to purple ray flowers and a rather small, bright yellow disk. The bracts are leaf-like, woolly, and in one row.

Lower leaves are stalked, to 3½" long, and lanceolate, whereas the upper ones are sessile and much reduced.

Grows around lakes and ponds, in moist meadows, and willow thickets.

Life Zones: Subalpine and Alpine

Flowering Time: June to August

Pinnate-Leaved Daisy

Erigeron pinnatisectus

Aster Family (Asteraceae)

Perennial, to 5" tall, in dense clumps, with erect, stout, curved stems.

Flower heads are single, to 1" across, with many lavender ray flowers, yellow disks, and hairy bracts.

Leaves are basal, to 3" long, stalked, and dissected into finger-like, hairy lobes.

Grows in meadows and boulder fields, and on rocky tundra, slopes, and ridges.

Life Zones: Subalpine and Alpine

Flowering Time: July and August

Showy Daisy

(Meadow Fleabane, Aspen Daisy)

Erigeron speciosus macranthus

Aster Family (Asteraceae)

Perennial, to 3' high, with shiny, twisting stems.

Flower heads to 1" across, with many lavender or pinkish ray flowers, yellow to tan disks, and a row of green and white bracts.

Leaves are lance-shaped, clasping, soft but leathery, to 3½" long.

Grows at the edges of woods and in clearings; common in aspen groves.

Life Zones: Foothills to Subalpine

Flowering Time: June to August

Subalpine Daisy

Erigeron peregrinus
(E. callianthemus, E. salsuginosus)

Aster Family (Asteraceae)

Perennial, to 20" tall, with erect, stout, curving stems that are hairy near the top.

Flower heads are large (to 1½" across), with purple to reddish ray flowers, bright yellow disks, and reflexed, purplish bracts.

Leaves are thick, narrowly lance-shaped to spatulate, and stalked; upper leaves are smaller, sessile.

Grows in moist meadows and tundra swales, along streams, and around ponds.

Life Zones: Subalpine and Alpine

Flowering Time: July and August

Three-Nerved Fleabane

Erigeron subtrinervis
(E. incanescens)

Aster Family (Asteraceae)

Perennial, to 3' tall, with stout, sticky, hairy stem that branches into slender branchlets near the top.

Flower heads are numerous, to 1" across, in one-sided bunches, with slender, purplish to pinkish rays, yellow, ½" disks, and sticky, reflexed bracts that have whitish margins.

Leaves are bright green, hairy, 3-veined, to 3" long, and stalked. Stem leaves are clasping and narrowly oval.

Grows in exposed sites, such as meadows and hillsides.

Life Zones: Foothills to Subalpine

Flowering Time: June to August

Common Harebell

(Scotch Harebell, Bluebell, Bellflower,
 Witches Thimble)

Campanula rotundifolia
(C. petiolata)

Bellflower Family
(Campanulaceae)

Perennial, to 2' tall, with
slender, erect, branched stems.

Flowers are bell-shaped, nodding,
to 1" long, with 5 lavender to
purple, fused petals that flare at
the tips and 5 short, spreading
sepals.

Leaves at the base are roundish,
oval, and wither early; upper
leaves are linear, to 3½" long,
and alternate.

Very common on grassy slopes,
in meadows and forest clearings,
at the edges of woods, and even
on grassy tundra.

Life Zones: Foothills to Alpine

Flowering Time: June to October

Purple Bellflower
(Parry Bellflower)
Campanula parryi
Bellflower Family (Campanulaceae)

Perennial, to 12" tall, with erect, slender stem.

Flowers are single, erect to tilted, broadly funnel-shaped, ½" long, and bluish purple, with the tips of the fused petals flaring out.

Lower leaves to 2 ½" long, stalked, and bristly; stem leaves are linear, ascending, and stalkless.

Grows in aspen groves, forest openings, and moist meadows, and on grassy slopes.

Life Zones: Montane and Subalpine

Flowering Time: July to September

Subalpine Larkspur

Delphinium barbeyi
(D. subalpinum, D. cockerelli)

Buttercup Family (Ranunculaceae)

Perennial, to 6' tall, in large colonies, with woody rootstock and leafy, hollow stems.

Flowers are fragrant, in terminal, spikelike cluster, with small, purple, white-margined petals and 5 deep purple sepals. Upper sepal has ⅜" long spur.

Leaves are large, smooth, and palmately cleft into 5 or 7 lobes that are divided into coarsely toothed segments.

Found in moist places, such as bogs, stream banks, meadows, seeps, ponds, and forest openings.

Life Zones: Subalpine and Alpine

Flowering Time: July and August

Alpine Kittentails

(Alpine Besseya)

Besseya alpina
(Synthris alpina)

Figwort Family
(Scrophulariaceae)

Perennial, to 6" tall, with stout, erect, curving stems.

Flowers are in terminal spike, with 2-lipped, purple to reddish corolla and whitish, woolly calyx.

Leaves are mostly basal, to 2" long, heart-shaped, thick, and woolly.

Common in tundra meadows and on talus slopes and boulder fields.

Life Zone: Alpine

Flowering Time:
July to September

Dusky Beardtongue

(Dark Beardtongue, Whipple Penstemon,
 Dusky Penstemon)

Penstemon whippleanus
(P. glaucus, P. arizonicus, P. puberulus,
P. metcalfei, P. pallescens, P. stenosepalus)

Figwort Family (Scrophulariaceae)

Perennial, to 2' tall, with slender, leafy stem.

Flowers are in nodding clusters, to 1½"
long, with 2-lipped, maroon to dark purple
or white corolla and pointed, sticky sepals.

Leaves are opposite, to 6" long; the lower
leaves are oval and stalked, and the upper
leaves are narrow and sessile.

Grows in exposed sites, such as moraines,
talus slopes, forest clearings, meadows, and
roadsides.

Life Zones: Subalpine and Alpine

Flowering Time: July to September

Hall's Beardtongue

(Hall's Penstemon, Hall's Alpine Beardtongue)

Penstemon hallii

Figwort Famlly (Scrophulariaceae)

Perennial, to 8" tall, with erect stems.

Flowers are in loose, one-sided clusters, with 2-lipped corolla that is purple to bluish, or pinkish, and sticky. Calyx lobes are translucent.

Leaves are thick, smooth, and narrow.

Grows in gravelly and rocky areas in meadows, on slopes, and along ridges.

Life Zones: Subalpine and Alpine

Flowering Time: July and August

Fringed Gentian

(Rocky Mountain Fringed Gentian,
 Western Fringed Gentian, Feather Gentian)

Gentianopsis thermalis
(Gentiana thermalis, G. elegans,
 Anthopogon thermalis)

Gentian Family (Gentianaceae)

Annual, to 16" tall, in clumps, with erect, smooth stems.

Flowers are striking, broadly tubular, to 2½" long, with a deep blue to purple corolla whose 4 lobes are reflexed and fringed, and 1" long, pointed sepals.

Leaves are opposite, to 2" long, with up to 4 pairs on a stem.

Grows in meadows and bogs, along streams, and at the edges of forests.

Life Zones: Montane and Subalpine

Flowering Time: July to September

Little Gentian

(Rose Gentian, Love Gentian,
 Northern Gentian, Amarella, Felwort)

Gentianella acuta
(G. amarella)

Gentian Family (Gentianaceae)

Annual, to 16" tall, with erect, curved, slender, angled, leafy stem.

Flowers are tubular, in clusters, with a pink to lavender (sometimes white) corolla that is usually 4-lobed and has a hairy fringe inside.

Leaves are opposite, sessile, oblong, to 1½" long.

Grows in shady, moist places, in aspen groves, willow thickets, forest openings, and swales, and along streams.

Life Zones: Foothills to Alpine

Flowering Time: June to September

Star Gentian

(Star Swertia, Felwort)

Swertia perennis
(S. scopulina, S. congesta,
S. palustris)

Gentian Family (Gentianaceae)

Perennial, to 18" tall, in clumps, with runners and slender, erect or leaning stem.

Flowers are star-shaped, in clusters; the petals are dark purple or reddish to bluish purple, spreading, and pointed, and the 5 sepals are spreading and green. The 5 long, stout stamens protrude.

Leaves are mostly basal, in a rosette, to 6" long, spatulate, and fleshy, with long stalks. Stem leaves are opposite and reduced.

Found in bogs, marshes, and meadows, and along pond shores and stream banks.

Life Zones: Montane to Alpine

Flowering Time:
July to September

Twisted Gentian

(Perennial Fringed Gentian,
 Fragrant Gentian)

Gentianopsis barbellata
(Gentiana barbellata)

Gentian Family (Gentianaceae)

Perennial, to 5" tall, with erect, leafy stems.

Flowers are tubular, to 2" long. Corolla is twisted, purple to pinkish lavender, and the calyx is angular, pale green, blue-streaked, and sharply pointed.

Leaves to 1½" long, thick, and spatulate.

Found on grassy slopes and in meadows.

Life Zones: Subalpine and Alpine

Flowering Time: August and September

Sticky Geranium

(Pink Geranium, Western Cranesbill)

Geranium viscosissimum

Geranium Family (Geraniaceae)

Perennial, to 3' tall, in clumps, with leafy, erect, twisted, sticky stems.

Flowers to 2" across, in loose clusters, with 5 sticky, lavender petals and 5 sticky, green to purplish sepals.

Leaves are sticky and deeply and palmately dissected into 5 or 7 lobes with toothed margins.

Common along roads, trails, and ditches, and in meadows and clearings.

Life Zones: Foothills and Montane

Flowering Time: May to August

Wild Geranium

(Cranesbill)

Geranium caespitosum caespitosum
(G. fremontii, G. parryi)

Geranium Family (Geraniaceae)

Bushy perennial, in clumps, to 30" long, with sprawling, hairy, leafy stems.

Flowers to 1½" across, with 5 lavender petals.

Leaves are palmately and deeply dissected into 5 to 7 toothed lobes.

Grows in dry areas, such as slopes, hillsides, rolling meadows, and openings in woods and forests.

Life Zones:
Foothills to Subalpine

Flowering Time:
May to August

Alpine Columbine

(Dwarf Columbine, Alpine Blue
Columbine, Dwarf Blue Columbine)

Aquilegia saximontana

Hellebore Family (Helleboraceae)

Perennial, to 8" tall, in bunches,
with erect, branched, hairless stem.

Flowers are drooping, small (¾"),
with 5 roundish, white petals that
have curved, blue spurs, and 5 purple
to blue, petal-like sepals.

Leaves are mostly basal and divided
into 3-lobed leaflets.

Found in rock crevices, on talus
slopes, and among cliffs and
boulders.

Life Zones: Subalpine and Alpine

Flowering Time: July and August

Spurless Columbine

*Aquilegia coerulea
daileyae*

Hellebore Family
(Helleboraceae)

Perennial, to 2' tall,
with erect, sticky,
branched, grooved
stems.

Flowers to 3" across, with 5
purple, white-clawed, roundish
petals that are short-spurred,
and 5 purple, pointed sepals.

Leaves are divided into lobed
leaflets that are smooth on top
and hairy beneath.

Grows in forest openings and
on slopes and hillsides.

Life Zones: Foothills to Alpine

Flowering Time: June to August

Monkshood

(American Monkshood, Western Monkshood,
 Wolfbane, Blue Monkshood, Aconite)

Aconitum columbianum
(A. insigne)

Hellebore Family (Helleboraceae)

Perennial, to 7' tall, with erect, slender, flexible,
shiny stems.

Flowers are in open raceme, with 5 showy, blue to
purple (occasionally white) sepals and 5 negligible
petals. Three of the petals are rudimentary, and the
other two are spurlike and hidden by the "hood,"
which is formed by the uppermost sepal.

Leaves to 8" across and deeply cut into jaggedly
toothed lobes.

Found in moist situations, such as wet meadows
and forest clearings, lake shores, springs, and
willow thickets.

Life Zones: Montane to Alpine

Flowering Time: June to September

Wild Jris

(Blue Flag, Western Blue Flag,
 Water Flag, Snake Lily, Rocky
 Mountain Iris, Fleur-de-Lis)

Iris missouriensis

Iris Family (Iridaceae)

Perennial, to 2' high, in large patches, with creeping rootstock and stout, fleshy stem.

Flowers are spectacular, to 4" across, with 3 showy, reflexed sepals that are bluish purple with yellow and orange streaks, 3 erect, pale blue petals, and 3 petal-like pistils.

Leaves to 20" long, swordlike, basal, tough, and flexible.

Grows in moist environments, such as meadows, seeps, ditches, stream banks, and mountain parks.

Life Zones: Foothills to Subalpine

Flowering Time: May to July

Skullcap

Scutellaria brittonii
(S. virgulata)

Mint Family (Lamiaceae)

Perennial, to 10" tall, with leafy, sticky, and hairy stems.

Flowers are in pairs, to 1¼" long, bluish purple, and 2-lipped; the lower lip is white-ribbed.

Leaves are opposite, narrowly oval, to 2" long, sticky and hairy on top, and smooth beneath.

Grows in fairly dry areas on slopes and hillsides, and in thickets and open woods.

Life Zones: Plains to Montane

Flowering Time: May to July

Alpine Milkvetch

(Alpine Vetch, Mountain Vetch, Mountain Locoweed, Milkvetch, Rattleweed)

Astragalus alpinus
(A. pauciflorus, A. astragalinus, Phaca alpina, P. astragalina, Tium alpinum)

Pea Family (Fabaceae)

Perennial, to 10" high, in patches, with creeping rootstock and slender, weak, erect to creeping, angular stems.

Flowers are in short clusters, to ½" long, with united, blackish, hairy sepals and a purplish, reddish, and whitish corolla.

Leaves are basal and pinnately dissected into ⅜" long leaflets.

Likes shade and moisture in meadows and forest glades, along streams, and under bushes.

Life Zones: Montane to Alpine

Flowering Time: June to August

Mountain Blue Violet

(Blue Violet, Purple Violet,
Early Blue Violet, Hook-Spur Violet)

Viola adunca
(V. montanensis, V. retroscabra)

Violet Family (Violaceae)

Perennial, to 5" high, in clumps, with slender, leafy, erect to leaning stems.

Flowers are single, nodding, to ¾" long, with 5 purple to bluish or pinkish petals (the lower one large and spurred) and 5 green to purple sepals.

Common but often overlooked in meadows, aspen groves, and forest glades, along roads, and around springs and streams.

Life Zones: Montane to Alpine

Flowering Time: April to August

Purple Fringe

(Purple Pincushion, Alpine Phacelia,
 Silky Phacelia, Scorpionweed)

Phacelia sericea

Waterleaf Family (Hydrophyllaceae)

Perennial, to 16" tall, in clumps, with stout, hairy stems.

Flowers are in spikelike cluster to 7" long, with ¼" long, bell-shaped, deep purple corolla and very hairy sepals. The long purple stamens are the "pins" of the pincushion.

Leaves are deeply and pinnately cut into silvery, hairy lobes.

Common along roads and trails, in disturbed soil, on sandy and gravelly slopes, in forest openings, and on talus slopes.

Life Zones: Montane to Alpine

Flowering Time: June to August

Glossary

I have substituted English for "botanese" wherever possible in this book. However, some botanical terms cannot be avoided—there simply are no English substitutes—and certain English terms have specific meanings in botany and, therefore, need to be defined. The following illustrations show typical and/or common flower and leaf types. For written descriptions, and for definitions of other terms used in this guide, see the list of terms that follows the illustrations.

SIMPLE FLOWER

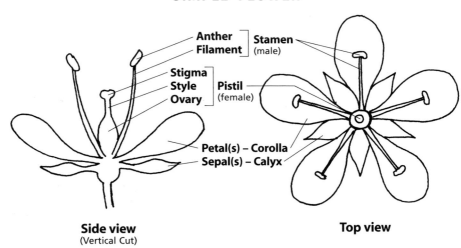

Anther ⎤ Stamen
Filament ⎦ (male)

Stigma ⎤
Style ⎥ Pistil
Ovary ⎦ (female)

Petal(s) – Corolla
Sepal(s) – Calyx

Side view
(Vertical Cut)

Top view

COMPOSITE FLOWER HEAD

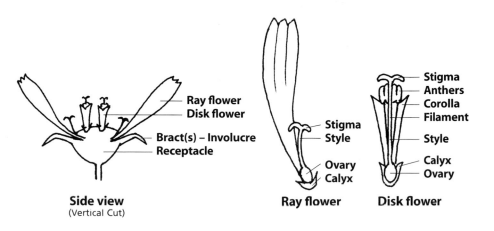

Ray flower
Disk flower

Bract(s) – Involucre
Receptacle

Side view
(Vertical Cut)

Stigma
Style

Ovary
Calyx

Ray flower

Stigma
Anthers
Corolla
Filament

Style

Calyx
Ovary

Disk flower

PEA FLOWER   GRASS SPIKELET

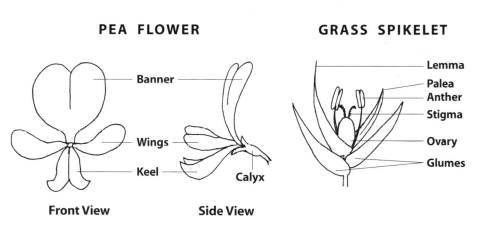

Banner

Wings

Keel

Calyx

Front View   **Side View**

Lemma
Palea
Anther
Stigma

Ovary

Glumes

INFLORESCENCES

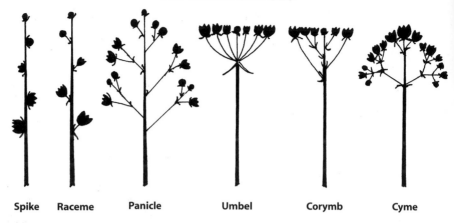

Spike   Raceme   Panicle   Umbel   Corymb   Cyme

SIMPLE LEAVES

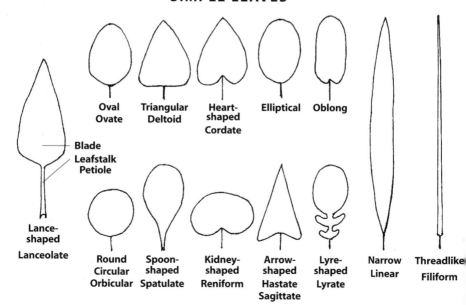

Oval
Ovate

Triangular
Deltoid

Heart-
shaped
Cordate

Elliptical

Oblong

Blade
Leafstalk
Petiole

Lance-
shaped
Lanceolate

Round
Circular
Orbicular

Spoon-
shaped
Spatulate

Kidney-
shaped
Reniform

Arrow-
shaped
Hastate
Sagittate

Lyre-
shaped
Lyrate

Narrow
Linear

Threadlike
Filiform

VENATION

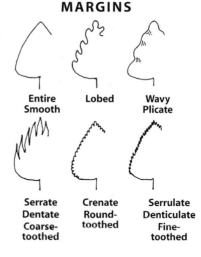

Pinnate
Featherlike

Palmate
Digitate
Fingerlike

Parallel

MARGINS

Entire
Smooth

Lobed

Wavy
Plicate

Serrate
Dentate
Coarse-
toothed

Crenate
Round-
toothed

Serrulate
Denticulate
Fine-
toothed

COMPOUND LEAVES

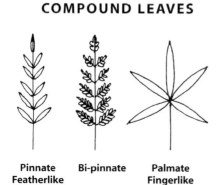

Pinnate
Featherlike

Bi-pinnate

Palmate
Fingerlike

LEAF ARRANGEMENT
on Stem, Branch or Twig)

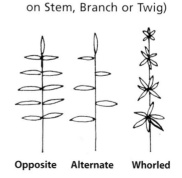

Opposite   Alternate   Whorled

LEAF ATTACHMENT

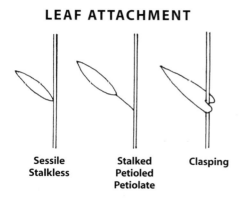

Sessile
Stalkless

Stalked
Petioled
Petiolate

Clasping

MISCELLANY

Tendril

Winged
Stalk

Clawed
Petal

Alternate One branch or leaf per node.

Annual A plant that lives one year.

Anther The flower organ that produces pollen.

Ascending Growing upward at an angle.

Awn A slender bristle or spine; used to describe grasses.

Axil The angle formed by a stem and its leaf.

Banner Upper, upright petal of a pea-type flower; also called the standard.

Biennial A plant that lives two years.

Bract A modified leaf below a flower or inflorescence.

Calyx Collective term for the sepals of a flower.

Claw Narrow stalk of petal.

Cleft Deeply cut.

Corm Thickened, vertical, underground stem.

Corolla Collective term for the petals of a flower.

Culm Stem of grasses, sedges, and rushes.

Decumbent Bent at the base, prostrate; usually used to describe stems.

Deltoid Triangular.

Entire Continuous margin of leaf, i.e., without lobes or teeth.

Fascicle Bundle of needles, spines, or bristles.

Filament Stalk supporting anthers.

Floret Small flower; used to describe grasses.

Glumes The two outer husks or bracts of a grass spikelet.

Hyaline Translucent, membranous.

Inflated Expanded, bulging, bloated.

Inflorescence Collective term for the flowers on a stem; cluster of flowers.

Involucre Ring of leaflike bracts below a flower cluster.

Keel Ridge or spine; the fused lower petals of a pea-type flower.

Krummholz Bent, stunted tree (usually at timberline)

Lanceolate Shaped like the head of a lance or spear.

Lemma Outer bract of a grass flower.

Lenticel Horizontal slit in bark.

Linear Narrow and long, with parallel margins.

Nerve Vein of leaf (or of other plant part)

Node The point on a stem where branches or leaves arise.

Opposite Branching in pairs.

Ovate Oval, egg-shaped.

Palea Inner bract of a grass flower.

Palmate Spreading like the fingers of a hand.

Panicle A much-branched inflorescence of stalked flowers.

Pedicel Flower stalk.

Peduncle Stalk of a flower cluster.

Perennial Plant that lives three years or longer.

Petiole Leaf stalk.

Pinnate Featherlike.

Pistil The seed-producing organ of a flower.

Raceme An inflorescence with stalked flowers along a stem.

Ray flower The outer flower of a composite flower head (used with Aster Family).

Reflexed Bent abruptly backward.

Rhizome Underground stem; rootstock.

Rootstock Underground stem; rhizome.

Rosette Ring or cluster of bracts or leaves; basal leaf cluster.

Scale Thin, transparent bract; used to describe sedges.

Sessile Without a stalk.

Spatulate Shaped like a spatula or spoon; narrowing toward the base.

Spike Inflorescence with stalkless flowers along a stem.

Spikelet Small flower cluster of grasses and sedges.

Stamen Male organ of a flower; consists of the filament and anthers.

Stigma The tip of the pistil where pollen is trapped.

Stipule Small, leaflike appendage at the base of a leaf.

Stolon A horizontal shoot that puts down roots; runner.

Style Stalklike part of the pistil.

Subtending Closely underlying or attached below; often used to describe bracts under a flower cluster.

Tendril Slender, clasping appendage (modified leaf or leaflet) that attaches a plant to something else.

Tepals Sepals and petals that are indistinguishable from each other.

Tuft Tight cluster of stems, bristles, or hairs; used to describe grasses and sedges.

Umbel Flower cluster whose stalks radiate from a common center.

Whorl Three or more leaves at one node.

Wing A thin, flat extension. Examples: winged stalk, winged fruit, winged seed. Also, one of the lateral petals of a pea-type flower.

Index of Common Names

Index of Latin Names

Selected References

Baerg, Harry J. *How to Know the Western Trees*, 2nd edition. Dubuque, Iowa: William C. Brown Company Publishers, 1973.

Beaudoin, Viola Kneeland. *The Beaudoin Easy Method of Identifying Wildflowers.* Aurora, Colorado: Evergreen Publishing Company, 1983.

Clements, Frederic F. and Clements, Edith S. *Rocky Mountain Flowers*. New York: Hafner Publishing Company, 1963.

Craighead, John J.; Craighead, Frank C. Jr.; and Davis, Ray J. *A Field Guide to Rocky Mountain Wildflowers*. Peterson Field Guide Series. Boston: Houghton Mifflin Company, 1963.

Cronquist, Arthur, et al. *Intermountain Flora, Vascular Plants of the Intermountain West*, Volumes 1-6. Bronx, New York: New York Botanical Garden, 1972-1994.

Duft, Joseph F. and Moseley, Robert K. *Alpine Wildflowers of the Rocky Mountains.* Missoula, Montana: Mountain Press Publishing, 1989.

Elias, Thomas S. *Trees of North America.* Outdoor Life/Nature Books. New York: Van Nostrand Reinhold Company, 1980.

Forey, Pamela. *Wild Flowers*. American Nature Guides. New York: Gallery Books, W. H. Smith Publishers, Inc., 1990.

Gould, Frank W. *Grasses of the Southwestern United States*. Tucson, Arizona: University of Arizona Press, 1973.

Harrington, H. D. *Manual of the Plants of Colorado.* Denver: Sage Books, 1954.

Hermann, Frederick J. *Manual of the Carices of the Rocky Mountains and Colorado Basin.* Agriculture Handbook No. 374. Washington, D.C.: U.S. Dept. Agriculture, 1970.

Kelly, George W. *A Guide to the Woody Plants of Colorado*. Boulder, Colorado: Pruett Publishing Company, 1970.

Kirkpatrick, Zoe Merriman. *Wildflowers of the Western Plains: A Field Guide.* Austin, Texas: University of Texas Press, 1992.

Nelson, Ruth Ashton, and Williams, Roger L. *Handbook of Rocky Mountain Plants.* Niwot, Colorado: Roberts Rinehart Publishers, 1992.

Orr, Robert T. and Orr, Margaret C. *Wildflowers of Western America.* New York: Alfred A. Knopf, Inc., 1974.

Pesman, M. Walter. *Meet the Natives.* 9th edition. Colorado: Denver Botanic Gardens & Roberts Rinehart Publishers, 1992.

Pohl, Richard W. *How to Know the Grasses.* Dubuque, Iowa: William C. Brown Company Publishers, 1953.

Porsild, A. E. *Rocky Mountain Wild Flowers*. Ottawa, Canada: National Museum of Canada, 1979.

Reynolds, William. *Wildflowers of America*. New York: Gallery Books, W. H. Smith Publishers Inc., 1987.

Rickett, Harold William. *Wild Flowers of the United States*, Volume 6, New York: McGraw-Hill Book Company, 1973.

Spellenberg, Richard. *The Audubon Society Field Guide to North American Wildflowers, Western Region*. New York: Alfred A. Knopf, 1987.

Strickler, Dee. *Prairie Wildflowers*. Columbia Falls, Montana: Flower Press, 1986.

————. *Forest Wildflowers*. Columbia Falls, Montana: Flower Press, 1988.

————. *Alpine Wildflowers*. Columbia Falls, Montana: Flower Press, 1990.

Venning, Frank D. and Saito, Manahu C. *A Guide to Field Identification, Wildflowers of North America*. New York: Golden Press, 1984.

Walcott, Mary Vaux; Platt, Dorothy Falcon; and Rickett, H. W. *Wildflowers of America*. New York: Crown Publishers, Inc., 1969.

Weber, William A. *Colorado Flora, Western Slope*. Boulder, Colorado: Associated University Press, 1987.

————. *Colorado Flora, Eastern Slope*. Niwot, Colorado: University Press of Colorado, 1990.

Willard, Bettie E., and Smithson, Michael T. *Alpine Wildflowers of the Rocky Mountains*. Estes Park, Colorado: Rocky Mountain Nature Association, 1988.

Williams, Jean, et al. *Rocky Mountain Alpines*. Portland, Oregon: Timber Press, 1986.

Wingate, Janet L. *A Simplified Guide to Common Colorado Grasses*. Privately published, 1986.

————. *Rocky Mountain Flower Finder*. Berkeley, California: Nature Study Guild, 1990.

Young, Robert G. and Young, Joann W. *Colorado West, Land of Geology and Wildflowers*. Salt Lake City, Utah: Artistic Printing Company, 1984.

Zwinger, Ann H. and Willard, Beatrice F. *Land Above the Trees*. New York: Harper and Row, Publishers, 1972.

ABOUT THE AUTHOR

PHOTO BY: BILL BURGER

Dr. G. K. "Joe" Guennel has lived in Colorado for 37 years and has made a name for himself in science and sports.

Born in Germany, Joe grew up in Pennsylvania and later moved to Indiana, where he attended Butler University in Indianapolis. During World War II, he served in the United States Army, with the infantry in 1944 and 1945 in France, Germany, and Austria. After the war, he worked for the U.S. military government as a civilian in Karlsruhe, West Germany, where he married Hilde E. Lang in 1947. He returned to Butler University to earn an M.S. degree in botany and later received a Ph.D. in botany from Indiana University.

For twelve years Joe worked for the Indiana Geological Survey, conducting research in palynology (the study of spores and pollen) and earning a worldwide reputation. He has been recognized in *American Men and Women of Science, Who's Who in the West,* and the international publication, *Men of Achievement.*

In 1961 Joe and Hilde moved to Colorado, where Joe joined Marathon Oil Company's Research Center in Littleton. Active in community sports as a coach and organizer, he is known as "the father of Colorado soccer" and is a member of the Colorado Sports Hall of Fame. He has been inducted into the National Soccer Hall of Fame in Oneonta, New York, for his work promoting soccer in the Midwest and Rocky Mountain region.

After retiring, Joe undertook an intensive study of the flora of Colorado, painting, photographing, and describing plants throughout the state, as well as cataloging slides and specimens he collected over the years while hiking and climbing. He has compiled and organized his work into this two-volume set, *Guide to Colorado Wildflowers.*